Confessions of a Private Eye

My Thirty Years Investigating

Cheaters, Frauds, Missing Persons and Crooks

BY SCOTT B. FULMER

FULMER, P.I. PRESS

SALT LAKE CITY, UTAH

The following story is true. I have attempted to recreate the events of the last thirty years in accordance with my notes, conversations with the participants, public records, news reports, video evidence, and my memory. Specific dialogue in the book comes from the same sources and does not represent word-for-word transcripts. Rather, I have retold them in a way that evokes the feeling and meaning of what was said at the time and in all instances, the essence of the dialogue is accurate. Apart from the mention of well-known public figures, all the names, locations, dates and certain other identifying details have been changed to protect the privacy of individuals. Any resemblance to real events or persons, living or dead, is purely coincidental.

Copyright © 2018 Scott B. Fulmer

All rights reserved. No part of this book may be used or reproduced in any manner whatsoever without written permission except in the case of brief quotations embodied in critical articles or reviews

ISBN-13: 978-1979693127
ISBN-10: 1979693129

FIRST EDITION

Printed in the United States of America

Editing and Proofreading by Valerie Fulmer and Courtney Southwick
Cover photographs courtesy of the author

For book orders and media appearances send your requests to scott@fulmerpi.com

Published by Fulmer, P.I. Press
Salt Lake City, Utah

For Jupiter, who fired the imagination of a young boy; Jim, who kept it alive; George, who set me on the path; and Jay, who set the standard.

And of course, Valerie. The love of my life and my greatest adventure. If I could, I would go back to the day we first met and stop time just to spend every moment with you.

CONTENTS

Acknowledgments   pg. v
Preface   pg. vii

1. The Kidnapping of Cruz Guzman   pg. 1

2. Raised on Rockford   pg. 15

3. Brothers in Arms   pg. 29

4. On the Job Training   pg. 44

5. The Investigator's Apprentice   pg. 59

6. Tricks of the Trade   pg. 73

7. George Bush and the Secret Government Cave   pg. 87

8. Dying with your Eyes Open   pg. 102

9. Your Security Clearance is Denied   pg. 116

10. Citizen Four and the Demise of USIS   pg. 131

11. The Missouri Compromise   pg. 145

12. You May All go to Hell and I will go to Texas   pg. 159

13. She's a Little Runaway   pg. 171

14. Truth is the First Casualty of Love   pg. 184

15. Do All Strippers Drive Cadillac Escalades?   pg. 200

16. Thieves, Frauds and Scams   pg. 215

17. Fulmer, P.I.   pg. 230

Notes   pg. 244

ACKNOWLEDGMENTS

I am grateful to my mother Evalyn J. Fulmer, a published author of numerous books, for her editing and guiding hand throughout the evolution of this book. Both her, and my father Harvey H. B. Fulmer provided background information on family history and past events. They are wonderful parents that always believed in me and encouraged me to pursue my dreams.

Thank you to my college mentor, James D. Calder, Ph.D., Professor of Political Science and Geography at the University of Texas at San Antonio.

Thank you to Phil Strand and Fern Cotton formerly of USIS. They remain some of the most professional investigators it has ever been my pleasure to work with. And thank you to Stephen J. Harris, formerly of the appellate division of the Missouri State Public Defender System.

A personal thank you to retired F.B.I. Special Agent and Texas private investigator Ricardo Martinez and his wife Karolyn for their kindness towards myself and Valerie. And yes, I always enjoyed the high school fundraisers!

Thank you to Dr. James D. Walker, institute scientist in the mechanical engineering division at Southwest Research Institute for the nuclear science tutorial. And Dr. Steven Redd, associate professor of political science in the College of Letters and Science at the University of Wisconsin, Milwaukee for the political science lessons.

And to my Army brother and mentor, U.S. Special Forces SFC Theodore Slaughter, U.S. Army (Retired), a snake-eater, heart-breaker and life-taker.

Everything I learned about leadership and determination, I learned from you. First Strike!

A special thank you to my sister Courtney A. Southwick for her indispensable editing of this manuscript and her advice.

And of course, to Valerie, my partner in life as well as in business. Your boundless patience and unwavering confidence in me has always given me wings to fly. Your advice, wise counsel and editing skills have helped make this book possible. I simply could not have lived my dream without your love and support. Thank you for sticking with me through the lean times. You believe in me.

And finally, to my beautiful children Brandon, Dylan and Alyssa who suffered through my many absences as I conducted investigations abroad. You are my greatest treasures. I know it was hard for you when I was away. But know this: wherever I was, whatever I was doing, you were always my first priority.

S.F.

Salt Lake City, Utah

PREFACE

I am a private spy for hire. To be more specific, I am a private eye. I conduct investigations for anyone willing to pay a fee. I work in the private sector although I have worked for both state and federal government. I carry a loaded Beretta 9mm in my waistband. I can tell you if there's a GPS tracker on your car, if your husband is seeing another woman and which employees are stealing from your company.

Ever since I could remember I've wanted to be a private detective. I came of age during the 1970's and early 1980's, stellar years for private investigators on television. Shows such as *The Rockford Files, Mannix, Magnum, P.I.,* and *Charlie's Angels* were popular. The list goes on and on. And remember, this was before cable television; we only had three channels.

My work has taken me all over the country. I've conducted surveillance on the Native American reservations of New Mexico and in the mountains and posh ski resorts of western Colorado. I've worked investigations in the dangerous neighborhoods of Houston and in north Omaha, Nebraska. From the streets of Compton to the streets of San Francisco; the historic neighborhoods of St. Louis to the affluent communities of north Dallas. From Texas to Nebraska and California to Washington, D.C. Not from a plush office in downtown New York City or a high-rise office building in Chicago, but from a secure office somewhere along the Wasatch Front near Salt Lake City. That's right, Utah. The Beehive State. Thirty-fourth in population. It's the birthplace of Donny and Marie Osmond and Beat generation writer Neal Cassady. With Valerie, my wife and Girl at my side, I have conducted investigations throughout the United States. The hustle and bustle never ends. I typically fly somewhere almost monthly, along with driving throughout Utah and the immediate surrounding states.

In a career spanning almost three decades I have been called on to handle a variety of investigations involving murder, suicide, kidnapping, fraud, rape, missing persons, inventory shortage and infidelity.

I have investigated cheating spouses and deadbeat dads. I've found runaways and investigated kidnappers, thieves, bigamists, drug dealers, and members of the FLDS Church. I've investigated members of the George W. Bush administration and people in trailer parks.

Over the years, I have been inundated with requests to tell my story. Friends, family, clients and even strangers seated next to me on my numerous flights have asked me to discuss these experiences. I've walked among the seedy underbelly of society and seen the face of evil. More often than not, it looks normal. Like your next-door neighbor, or someone you'd serve with in the PTA.

My experiences have changed me profoundly. I rarely trust people I don't know, mostly because I know what people are capable of. I'm more cynical than I'd like to be. But through it all, I've helped people. I've made a difference. I've provided solutions and peace of mind. I have uncovered fraud, recovered children and exposed dishonesty and I'd like to think somehow made the world a better place. After almost thirty years of helping people, I finally put pen to paper to share my experiences.

Here are my stories…

CHAPTER 1

THE KIDNAPPING OF CRUZ GUZMAN

The game is afoot! The parents of seven-year-old Cruz Guzman could not get along. Although they were divorced and shared custody of their young son, the difficulties and the acrimony continued unabated. The real problem in this domestic disaster was Cruz's mother, Dolores Guzman; a beautiful, thirty-year-old woman with a stunning, voluptuous figure, an absolutely flawless almond complexion and long silky black hair. In Spanish, the name Dolores means sorrows, which was appropriate because she was causing enough sorrow for everyone involved. I have conducted enough of these types of investigations to know that the problem could have easily been the father. However, in this case it was the mother causing all the heartache.

Dolores was unstable on a good day and totally out of control when she freely mixed alcohol with prescription drugs. She was verbally and emotionally abusive to her ex-husband Pablo, a quiet and reserved accountant, and even to their son Cruz, a shy, second grader. These issues and many others became the basis for their eventual divorce. She was just plain mean and vindictive. Suffice it to say, the issues were so alarming the family law judge granted Pablo full custodial rights and Dolores limited visitation. Of course, this did not sit well with Dolores. After the divorce, she reluctantly moved in with her sister Lourdes in an aging apartment complex in Midvale, Utah surrounded by beautiful white Aspen trees. It was there she began to hatch her plan. Although Pablo didn't know it at the time, Dolores had decided to do what many non-custodial parents do. She would violate the court order and take her son. She couldn't allow Cruz to live with anyone but her.

On a cool and crisp fall morning in September Dolores and her younger brother Maximillian drove to the local elementary school where Cruz was sitting in Ms. Winder's second grade class. Max turned his bright blue compact car into an empty space near the front of the parking lot and turned off the engine. Both he and Dolores sat quietly for a moment without saying a word. It was Dolores who finally broke the silence. "Alright, let's go" she said. They both exited the vehicle and slowly climbed the stairs to the front of the school. They walked past the school office where visitors were required to sign in straight to Cruz's classroom. Ms. Winder was in the middle of a spelling lesson. She was startled when Max suddenly opened the door open and stood there. Without uttering a word Dolores rushed past him to Cruz's desk. A startled Ms. Winder asked, "May I help you?"

Dolores remained eerily silent. Ms. Winder would later remark to the Unified Police Department that Dolores appeared dedicated and singular in her purpose. Max, on the other hand, stood nervously by the classroom door with his hands in his pockets looking every bit the unwilling participant. He continually peered out in the hallway as if he expected the police to materialize at any moment. Without hesitation Dolores grabbed Cruz by the arm and began dragging him out of the classroom. He went along willingly. After all, she was his mother. Ms. Winder quickly got on the phone and called the front office to alert the principal. She was aware that Pablo had custody and had spoken to him about the serious issues he was having with his ex-wife. Even so, she had no idea who Dolores was.

After receiving Ms. Winder's frantic call, Benslee Smoot, the school principal, instructed her secretary to telephone the police immediately. Smoot then moved to intercept Dolores and Max as they exited the school and began walking towards the parking lot with Cruz. She ran after them yelling, "The police are on the way!" She then added, "You're not taking that boy out of here!" She broke into a jog and quickly closed the distance between herself and Dolores. Smoot then lunged forward attempting to grab Cruz's arm. Max was already behind the wheel of the vehicle and had started the engine. He began yelling, "Let's go, let's go!" Just as Ms. Smoot reached out to grab Cruz's arm, Dolores wheeled back and punched her squarely in the face. Dolores then pushed Cruz into the back seat of the car, jumped in after him and slammed the car door. It was at this point, witnessing the violence between his mother and his school principal, that Cruz began to cry. With the faint sound of police sirens closing in the distance, Max floored the gas pedal spewing gravel in the air as Ms. Smoot sat down on the parking lot nursing a bloody nose. And with that, Max, Dolores and Cruz disappeared into thin air somewhere in the vast Salt Lake valley.

Once Pablo was notified of the situation he, too, telephoned the police. And while the police did try to locate Dolores and Cruz, they eventually reached a dead end. In fact, the investigating detective periodically called Pablo to ask if he had heard anything. And so, the days turned into weeks and the weeks became months as Pablo grew increasingly despondent over the situation. After Cruz's birthday came and went without so much as a telephone call, Pablo began to lose hope that he would ever see his son again. Since the police had not been successful in finding Cruz, the normally reticent Pablo turned to his parents for answers. Raul and

Hortencia Guzman, Cruz's grandparents, resolved that something proactive had to be done. And that's when they decided to hire a private investigator.

Cruz had been missing for about three months by the time I became involved. As a parent of three children myself, I couldn't begin to imagine what Pablo and his parents were going through. I was asked to help find young Cruz and bring him home. I wish I could tell you this kind of thing is easy but it's not. It's expensive, time consuming and often full of dead ends. I had few leads to go on, and Dolores already had a three-month head start. The most promising lead was an address for Dolores' sister, Lourdes, in Midvale. So that's exactly where I started.

Midvale was originally known as Bingham Junction when it was settled in the mid to late 1800's. Some twelve miles south of Salt Lake City, it was two events that would put Midvale on the map; the coming of the Union Pacific railroad and the discovery of silver in nearby Bingham Canyon and Little Cottonwood Canyon. For now, Midvale was the center of my investigation. I learned from Pablo that Dolores and her sister Lourdes were very close. To make matters worse and cause even further confusion, I learned that Lourdes had a son who bore a striking resemblance to Cruz and was about the same age. I began by conducting surveillance on Lourdes at her apartment in the hopes that Dolores lived there or would visit with Cruz in tow. If she showed up without Cruz I could at least place a commercial grade GPS tracker on her vehicle in the hopes she would eventually lead us to her son's location. It was a difficult apartment complex to surveil for a couple of reasons. First, Lourdes' unit was in the back of the complex facing an open field. Second, the apartment was primarily filled with lower income tenants many of whom were involved in drug use or other petty crimes; the kir who are naturally suspicious. Additionally, many of the residents were or on disability. As a result, they were home regularly and were very keen to any person or vehicle that did not belong there. It was an older complex. The exterior paint on most of the buildings was peeling and in need of a paint job. Moreover, it was evident the complex lacked any regular basic maintenance. The landscape needed attention as well. Someone had placed a stained, bright green couch with a missing seat cushion in front of one of the garbage dumpsters. Several of the cars in the parking lot were on blocks or looked as if they hadn't been moved in months.

I set up a surveillance position outside the apartment complex with another investigator. As luck would have it, there was only one way in and out. But unfortunately, the apartment complex exited on to a very busy road. If Dolores left, we would have to be on her immediately. Otherwise we would risk losing her in traffic. The problem with this situation was that we would more than likely draw unwanted attention to ourselves.

We ended up following Lourdes a couple of times when she left but she was always alone or with a man we didn't recognize. In all of our efforts at Lourdes' apartment, we never caught sight of Dolores or Cruz. Everywhere we turned seemed to be just another dead end.

About a month later I finally got a promising lead. I cannot reveal to you how I found out because it would compromise confidential sources and key methods I use in these types of cases. Suffice it to say, in cases involving missing children or runaways I spend a great deal of time talking to people on the periphery of the subject's life. In doing so, I learned Dolores would more than likely be at a particular business address in downtown Salt Lake City on a specific day. There was no guarantee she would actually show up or have Cruz with her. However, if she did we would attempt to recover the child. If she didn't we would at least attempt to place a tracker under her car in the hopes she would eventually lead us to Cruz. We would then call local law enforcement who would recover the child.

The possibilities were nerve-wracking. There was little room for error. If we were unable to place a tracker on Dolores' car or we lost her during the moving surveillance in downtown Salt Lake City, we'd be back at square one. If she discovered us attempting to install the tracker or became aware we were following her, it could seriously jeopardize the investigation. And if that happened, we might never see Cruz again. Unlike how private eyes are depicted on television, the real work can be much more difficult.

In the meantime, Raul and Hortencia were understandably growing impatient. The investigation had been going on for months. They had paid us a lot of money and so far, we hadn't produced any tangible results. They seemed to be losing hope.

Eventually the day arrived to conduct our stakeout of the office building in Salt Lake City. It was a cold but sunny winter day. I normally work alone, but due to the nature of this particular case I brought along an associate, Ken Roberts. Ken is tall, barrel-chested, and blessed with equal measures of bravery and competence. He's a former EMT with a keen intellect and a great person to have next to you in a crisis. He would be my extra set of eyes and ears on this caper.

We met Pablo in the parking lot of a Greek restaurant in the downtown area less than three blocks from where Dolores would have her appointment. We stood next to our cars and shivered in the cold as we briefly discussed the procedures, expectations and possible outcomes of what we were about to do. Then we synchronized our watches (really) and all three of us left in separate vehicles and drove to the office building where we were expecting Dolores. We quickly moved our vehicles into position in the parking lot and then waited.

Normally, I would never involve the client in the actual surveillance. That's a recipe for disaster. But given the fact that Lourdes' son looked similar to Cruz, I needed Pablo to make a positive identification. Otherwise, Ken or I could end up grabbing the wrong child. If that happened, we would find ourselves arrested and behind bars for attempted kidnapping.

As I sat in the parking lot my stomach felt like it was tied in knots. I peered through the rear window of my van, attempting to identify the occupants of every vehicle that arrived. Although I had a picture of both Dolores and Cruz, I was counting on Pablo to recognize them. In general, things don't happen in real-life like they do on television. Even with a photograph people can be difficult to identify. They change their hair style or lose or gain weight. Sometimes they just don't look like their picture. It didn't help that the parking lot was crowded and that there were two possible entry points. As people came and went it soon became a challenge to get a good look at each of them. The plan was for Pablo to call me with a confirmation once he saw Dolores and determined whether Cruz was with her. If he was, we would make our move.

I continued to wait and my cell phone remained silent. I must've checked the ringer volume a hundred times, afraid I would miss his call. As I sat there the minutes slowly turned into hours. After a couple of hours had gone by, I began to consider the possibility that my source was wrong. Maybe Dolores had come and gone and we had missed her? Maybe she had come yesterday. Perhaps she was coming tomorrow? I imagined a multitude of scenarios and none of them provided me any comfort. I began to feel that familiar pain in my gut. That nervousness that I sometimes felt when a surveillance wasn't going the way it should. Despite the chilly winter day, I broke into a cold sweat and started to feel nauseated. And that's when I saw her. Plain as day. And she looked exactly like her picture.

A white Nissan Maxima with tinted windows arrived and moved into a parking space several cars down from my vehicle but out of my direct view. Two women, a man and a child exited the vehicle, crossed the parking lot and began to ascend the stairs to the office building in front of me. I immediately recognized both Dolores and her sister Lourdes. The man, who I assumed to be Dolores' brother Max, followed several steps behind them. Walking next to Dolores was a young boy about four feet tall, however I had not seen his face. It was either Cruz or it was Lourdes' son. By the time I processed this information they had climbed to the top of the stairs and disappeared into the building. I looked down at my phone and it had remained silent. Still no telephone call from Pablo. Surely, he had seen them. I picked up my phone and got him on the line. Apparently, Dolores and company had arrived and entered the office building so quickly that he had somehow missed them. I told him to sit tight and keep his eyes glued on the front door of that office building. We couldn't make our move until Pablo confirmed that the young boy was his son. I then called my associate Ken and filled him in. He had missed them too but was now watching the large glass doors of the office building like a hawk. I ended my call, sat back and breathed a sigh. And I began to wait again. I was suddenly very thirsty. I could feel butterflies in my stomach. My adrenal glands were on overload, however there was nothing more to do but wait a little longer.

About twenty minutes later a young boy exited the building and hopped down the stairs by himself. Within seconds my cell phone rang. As I picked it up I noticed Dolores, Lourdes and Max exiting the building. It was Pablo on the phone. "It's him" he said. "What do I do?" I had him immediately pull his car up right behind Dolores' Nissan effectively blocking her in. He then jumped out and grabbed Cruz and lifted him up. Father and son embraced. A huge smile broke out on Cruz's face as he recognized his father. As I watched this scene from my surveillance vehicle twenty feet away I remember saying out loud "Get out of here Pablo! Go, go, go!" But Pablo hesitated just a bit too long. As he turned to get back in his car with Cruz, it was obvious Dolores had recognized him. She ran to his car and reached in grabbing the keys out of the ignition. Then with a fake smile and a hint of derision she dropped the keys down the front of her blouse between her ample cleavage. Dolores then tried to pull Cruz away from his father. "Stop!" Pablo said. "You're hurting him." Things were about to escalate out of control. If only Pablo had quickly driven away rather than hesitated.

Pablo had his phone pressed to his ear with his shoulder as he held Cruz. I called and told him the police were already on their way and to just hang in there. I gave him further instructions and he moved towards his car. He placed Cruz on the hood of the car and stood next to him with his arms wrapped around the young boy. Father and son were holding on to each other for dear life. They would stay in that position for several minutes until the police arrived.

Because Dolores had grabbed the keys we had a tense standoff. We couldn't grab Pablo and Cruz without risking a physical altercation with Dolores, Lourdes and Max. Ken and I remained nearby but did not make our presence immediately known fearing our intervention would raise the tension level and cause additional problems. If Dolores became violent then we would have no choice but to intervene. For some reason she remained fairly calm. She spoke with Pablo trying to convince him that Cruz was better off with her. I recognized this was our one and only chance to recover Cruz. If we failed, there wouldn't be a second chance. I instinctively reached into my backpack and grabbed a GPS tracker and clutched it tightly in my hand only to let it go moments later. I realized the opportunity to place it on Dolores' vehicle had come and gone.

The Salt Lake City Police arrived in exactly twelve minutes. In the meantime, Ken had also called the Utah Department of Child and Family Services (DCFS). Once the police arrived Ken and I exited our surveillance vehicles and walked over to where Pablo was holding Cruz. Dolores was both startled and puzzled by our sudden appearance. She was on a cell phone call and pacing frantically, unsure of what to do. Max stood there with a dumbfounded look on his face. Although he had participated in taking Cruz from school several months prior, it was clear he had no stomach for any further confrontations.

Several police officers exited their vehicles and approached to surmise the situation. I immediately identified myself to the police as a licensed private investigator and showed them my credentials. I identified Ken as my associate and Pablo as the client. I explained that we were the good guys and that Dolores had violated a court order by taking Cruz months ago. I handed a certified copy of the court documentation to the police officer. It reflected Pablo as the custodial parent. As I was explaining what had happened and pointing out the parties involved, the lead officer said "Alright. Hold on. Stand over there." He pointed to where my vehicle was parked. Evidently, he wasn't impressed. By this time, the DCFS investigator had also arrived. Her name was Amber and, although she was a petite woman in her early twenties, she possessed an air of authority. The police immediately separated everyone. Ken and I stood next to our surveillance vehicles. One of the officers handcuffed Pablo and placed him in the back of a patrol car. The sudden use of the handcuffs concerned me. This is not how I pictured the day ending. I watched as Dolores and Cruz were placed in separate patrol cars. I identified myself to Amber and also gave her a certified copy of the court documentation. Like the police officer before her, she didn't seem too impressed. Ken and I watched as she began going to each police car, one at a time. First, she interviewed Pablo, then Dolores and finally young Cruz. While I was standing there waiting, Ken had a short conversation with one of the police officers and then walked back over to fill me in. He said the police viewed the situation as a civil matter. This didn't really come as a surprise. At first, they were hesitant to get involved but they eventually decided to defer to whatever decision the DCFS investigator made.

After what seemed like an eternity, but in reality was only about twenty minutes, I observed the lead police officer having a short conversation with Amber. I couldn't hear a word from where I was standing. He suddenly barked an inaudible command to the officer who had Pablo in his car. That officer pulled Pablo out, removed the handcuffs and escorted him over to the police car where Cruz was sitting. Cruz jumped out of the police cruiser and ran into his father's open arms. I exhaled deeply. It felt as if I had been holding my breath the entire time. Perhaps this day was going to end well after all.

Based on the court documentation we had provided and her interviews with Pablo, Dolores and Crus, Amber recommended that the police release Cruz to his father, which they promptly did. Now it was time for us get the heck out of Dodge. I asked the police to hold on to Dolores for a few minutes to give us a head start. Pablo put Cruz in his car and then followed me out of the parking lot. Ken pulled in behind him and we got out of the area as fast as we could. The last thing I saw in my rear-view mirror was an angry and disgruntled Dolores flailing her arms and arguing with one of the police officers.

We drove several miles down the road and pulled into a fast food restaurant on 400 South near the University of Utah. Once inside, father and son got reacquainted while we awaited the arrival of Pablo's parents. It was shortly after our arrival that Cruz told his father he had not been attending school during his absence. In fact, he had been living with his mother and some other people, whom he did not know, at a house somewhere in Mexico. Everyone in the house spoke Spanish. Since Cruz only spoke English he could not provide any further details. That certainly explained why he was so difficult to locate. It was also the first time since our little adventure that I began to allow myself to relax. But I still found myself continually looking out the window expecting Dolores to arrive at any moment.

I wish I could've videotaped the moment Cruz's grandparents arrived. As Raul and Hortencia entered the restaurant Cruz ran to his grandmother. She promptly swept him up in her arms and held him tightly as if she would never let him go. There were plenty of tears and kisses that day. As I watched this sweet reunion I realized that, as a private investigator, what I do has real-life consequences. Clients rely on my professional advice and my experience to help them overcome their problems and find peace of mind in a troubled world. I found myself feeling grateful that this case had ended so well.

According to the National Center for Missing and Exploited Children (NCMEC)i, the majority of missing children can be classified as endangered runaways. The second most common type involves the kidnapping of children by non-custodial parents or other relatives. In these types of cases, the majority of the time the perpetrator turns out to be the mother, as it was with Dolores Guzman. Fortunately, abductions by strangers are very rare, only comprising about one percent according to the NCMEC.

The kidnapping of Cruz Guzman by his mother was a very difficult ordeal for the family, nevertheless, it had a happy ending. Before they left, Cruz's grandmother embraced me. In almost thirty years as a private investigator I have never been hugged by a client. She looked up at me with tears in her eyes and in her limited English thanked Ken and I for recovering her grandson. She then said some things in Spanish I didn't understand. But it didn't matter. I could see the message in her eyes. It was a tender moment I have always cherished and have reflected on again and again.

CHAPTER 2

RAISED ON ROCKFORD

I always knew I wanted to be a private eye. I'm the oldest of nine children and the only boy. My parents worked very hard to provide and care for us. It couldn't have been easy with such a large family. As a result, we moved often; about four times between the time I attended third grade and when I started high school. Four different houses in four different neighborhoods and six different schools to get used to. If I had been an introvert I don't think I would've survived. Fortunately, I was gregarious and outgoing like my mother and I made friends easily. Still, the moves were tough, and they became increasingly difficult as I grew older.

I grew up in the late 1970's and the early 1980's; in between two celebrated decades. As a result, I've always felt somewhere in the middle. Almost as if I didn't entirely belong in either decade. Each year I was forced to start over and make new friends in my neighborhood and at school. It was during this time, I found solace in books. From an early age my mother nurtured in me and my sisters a love of reading. Each month she would board a city bus with all of us in tow and take us to a branch of the local public library. I would quickly disappear behind the tall bookshelves and emerge hours later with a stack of books that were frequently over the allowed limit one person could check out. As a result, I was reading on an adult level by third grade. With the arrival of each new school year I headed immediately to the school library. I lived in the fiction section where the mysteries were shelved. It was on those crowded dusty shelves that I first discovered *The Hardy Boys*ii and *Encyclopedia Brown*iii. I even read a few *Nancy Drew Mysteries*iv. I tried to solve the cases before the characters did, looking for clues and trying to make sense of it all. I had then, as I do now, an unquenchable desire to gather facts and information; to know and learn everything I could. I discovered that even in fiction books people are creatures of habit. They establish patterns and basic routines that become predictable; something that would serve me well years later when I became a private detective.

My two favorite book series were Sir Arthur Conan Doyle's *The Adventures of Sherlock Holmes* and Robert Arthur Jr.'s *The Three Investigators*.v With Sherlock Holmes I discovered a strict attention to detail and the need to learn and memorize a myriad of facts and principles. I was drawn to the amazing intellect and the use of logic and science by the world's greatest consulting detective. *The Three Investigators* was a series of books that involved the adventures of Jupiter Jones, Pete Crenshaw and Bob Andrews, three eager youths who solved baffling mysteries in and around Hollywood, California. Jupiter's parents had died in an automobile accident, so he was raised by his Uncle Titus and Mathilda Jones. They owned a salvage yard. Buried deep under the piles of scrap metal and forgotten over time was a small house trailer which served as the headquarters for the Three Investigators. Their cases involved what first appeared to be supernatural phenomena, such as a haunted mirror or a talking skull. But soon Jupiter, along with the aid of his friends Pete and Bob, would solve the mystery in much the same way Sherlock Holmes did. I remember staying up well past my bedtime reading one of these books with a flashlight underneath my blanket. Indeed, wherever I could be found I would more than likely have my nose in a book.

Each new year brought with it the excitement and thrilling anticipation that although I was enduring yet another painful move and would have to start over making new friends, surely my new school library would have additional volumes of these exciting mysteries that I had yet to read. I recall the eagerness and the delight I felt searching those library shelves. I remember walking down the aisles, my fingertips brushing past the book spines where the Dewey Decimal numbers were listed. And the sheer joy I felt when I stumbled upon one of the volumes I had yet to read. To this day, I can still remember how the books smelled.

Along with reading mysteries I remember lying on our frayed shag carpet in the 1970's watching the exciting capers of the intrepid Jim Rockford on *The Rockford Files*. We purchased our first Curtis Mathes color television set when I was 13 years old and it really made the show come alive. The Emmy Award winning series ran from 1974 to 1980.vi The show involved the exploits of James Scott Rockford, titular head of the one-man Rockford Agency; a private investigation company that specialized in closed casesvii. The Emmy and Golden Globe Award winning actor and Oklahoma native James Garner convincingly portrayed Rockford, a grouchy ex-con and private eye with a heart of gold.

On October 20, 1978, *The Rockford Files* aired an episode called *White on White and Nearly Perfect*. This episode included a young, thirty-two-year-old actor by the name of Tom Selleck as Lance White, P.I.; a handsome, successful private eye who seemed every bit the opposite of Rockford. Of course, Selleck would go on to fame in *Magnum, P.I., Blue Bloods* and several Jesse Stone made for television movies, as well as countless other films and television appearances.

Interestingly, I would later find that *The Rockford Files* was somewhat accurate in its portrayal of real-life private detectives. Jim never became wealthy, but he seemed to make just enough money to get by. He occasionally worked several cases pro bonoviii, although it was usually due to the incessant prodding of either his father Rocky or his lawyer Beth Davenport. Like real private investigators, he used several interesting aliases each season, often claiming to be Jim Taggart from the county tax office or Jimmy Joe Meeker, an oil speculator from Oklahoma. If you can get past the 1970's décor, fashions and kitschy music, you'll find the show has aged quite well.

Notwithstanding my love of mysteries and private investigator television shows, I soon discovered that criminal justice was also in the Fulmer family blood. My grandmother, Mildred Cain, worked for the San Antonio Police Department for fifteen years, first in the crime lab developing grisly crime scene photographs and then as a dispatcher. She later worked at the Bexar County Jail where she was a jail matron guarding female inmates. My grandmother would often accompany these women, whom she lovingly referred to as "my girls," to the county hospital where they gave birth or were treated for any number of medical issues.

Although she was a loving grandmother to my eight younger sisters and I, Grandma Cain was also tough. She had to be, to work in what was essentially a male dominated occupation at the time. She was raised in South Texas during the Great Depression. She once caught a pigeon that had landed on her window sill. She cooked it up and the family ate it because there was no other food in the house. She rolled her own cigarettes and drank Lone Star Longnecks right out of the bottle. We visited her almost every weekend when I was a child. She lived in a large home on the south side of San Antonio right off South Presa Street. We often gathered pecans that had fallen from two large pecan trees in her front yard. We would spend the whole day there and, if we were really lucky, she would make her famous enchiladas. She would often send me to fetch her a cold beer or her tobacco and rolling paper.

My grandmother had wanted to be a police officer, but this was the 1960's and that occupation was unfortunately not open to women at the time. I think she would've been an exceptional police officer. She had a huge poster of Humphrey Bogart on her bedroom wall; a reminder of his great role as private detective Sam Spade in the 1941 John Huston directed film, *The Maltese Falcon*. After she passed away my Aunt Sally made sure I was given her Bexar County Detention Officer's badge. I still have it. The gold shield bears badge number 154. It is framed and in a place of honor on my office wall. I often look up at it and think about her. I'd like to think that she would be proud of me and of my career as a private eye.

Grandma Cain wasn't the only family member in the criminal justice field. When I was 16-years-old my uncle, George Patrick Cain, became a licensed private investigator in Texas. He leased a small one-room office near the intersection of Goliad Road and E. Southcross Boulevard on the southeast side of San Antonio and opened for business. If he wasn't there he could be found down the street holding court at his favorite donut shop where he often ate breakfast and met clients. Having an uncle who is a private eye is about the coolest thing you could think of when you're a teenager. I remember sitting in his office with him and my aunt Shielda. He had his feet propped up on his desk as he regaled us with stories of interesting cases. At the time, he had a case that involved an attractive femme fatale, as he described her. George said she walked into his office in a low-cut, tight red dress, plopped down five crisp one-hundred-dollar bills and asked him for help finding her missing husband. It was the kind of thing that happened on *The Rockford Files* each week.

I couldn't wait to be a private eye like uncle George. He had a brown felt fedora perched atop a hat stand in the corner of his office near the door. A .38 caliber revolver also hung from the hat stand, snug in a soft leather shoulder holster. Although I was too young to be licensed he took me along on a couple of surveillance jobs. I remember sitting in his pickup truck with the windows rolled down eating a Whataburger[ix] and drinking an ice-cold bottle of Dr. Pepper he had bought for me. We watched and waited for the subject to arrive at their residence. I'm sure he was bored to tears, but I was sitting on the edge of my seat with anticipation. The feeling was electric. I felt a sense of possibility; that somehow, I was on the verge of solving some great caper. To this day, I still feel that same rush of adrenaline when a subject departs and I initiate a moving surveillance.

One day during a similar surveillance George handed me a small paperback book that would change my life forever. "I got this for you." He said. "I thought you might like it." It was a worn, mass-market used paperback from Avon books published in 1977 entitled, *Jay J. Armes, Investigator: The Astonishing True Story of the World's #1 Private Eye and Real-Life Six-Million Dollar Man*.[x] I had never heard of Jay J. Armes. But to say that I was hooked would be an understatement. I devoured the book in a weekend and have since re-read it numerous times.

Armes is a real-life, internationally-famous El Paso, Texas private investigator and generally regarded as one of the world's most successful private eyes. He is an absolute legend in the private investigator community. Speaking of being hooked, Armes had an accident as a child when he and an older boy, Dick Caples, got a hold of a box of railroad torpedoes. Unfortunately, both of Armes' hands were blown off as he attempted to open them. As a result, his hands were amputated above the wrists and he was fitted with a couple of prosthesis or hooks; hence, the Six-Million Dollar Man reference. Armes would go on to become a private investigator and work for celebrities, politicians, royalty and businessmen. His most famous case involved the recovery of actor Marlon Brando's kidnapped son, Christian Brandoxi, from Baja Mexico in 1972. Armes also claims to have landed a helicopter inside the courtyard of a Mexican prison where he scooped up two falsely accused U.S. citizens and ferried them back across the border to the U.S. This case was said to have inspired the 1975 Charles Bronson movie, *Breakout*.[xii] He has worked for several well-known individuals such as Elizabeth Taylor, Yoko Ono and Howard Hughes, to name a few. Armes also did some acting and played an assassin named Stoner in *Hookman*, the first episode of season six of *Hawaii Five-O* in 1973.

Sadly, my uncle George would pass away several years later after a short, courageous battle with a rather aggressive form of cancer. The cancer was discovered when he saw a doctor about a persistent neck ache that refused to go away. A U.S. Army Vietnam veteran, he was treated at the Audie L. Murphy VA Hospital in San Antonio where I took him for his weekly chemotherapy treatments. Unfortunately, by the time the cancer was discovered it was already well in the advanced stages. It had spread throughout his body and the doctors said there wasn't much they could do except try to make him comfortable. His final weeks were spent at home with his young son Gregory as the cancer swiftly ravaged his body. His wife Shielda had recently died in a tragic automobile accident. I, along with my mother, Evalyn, and my aunt Lelia Ferguson, took turns stopping by every day to attend to his needs and try to lift his spirits. It became increasingly difficult to find something positive to talk about during those visits. He was, for all intents and purposes, in hospice at his apartment. I guess I just didn't realize it at the time. I grew increasingly despondent as I saw him suffer. I wish I could've done more. George, along with my uncles Mike and William, the latter whom we affectionately called Bubba, were like the older brothers I never had. We all have our own personal flaws, and those who knew George were aware of his, but I'll always be grateful to him for introducing me to the private investigator business and for the gift of a simple used paperback book.

The Armes autobiography pretty much sealed my career goal. What had initially started out as a strong interest now became my overriding passion. I would become a private detective like Jay J. Armes and uncle George. Fast forward thirty years later, in 2007, and I happened to be traveling through El Paso on the way to Arizona. I stopped in for a few minutes and had an opportunity to meet both Armes and his son, Jay J. Armes, III, in their offices on Montana Street. It was surreal. Both Armes and his son were nothing but kind and gracious to me. He signed my first edition hardback copy of *Jay J. Armes, Investigator*, and even posed for a picture with me. And yes, I even shook his hook.

I eventually came to the decision that a college degree in criminal justice would lay the perfect foundation for my eventual career as the world's second greatest private eye. Money to attend college, however, was another matter. Family resources were limited. In fact, it would be my mother, Evalyn Joy Cain, who would be the first in the family to earn a college degree. She was born at home in San Antonio in 1942 and is a third-generation Texan. Her grandfather, Patrick Lee Cain, was born there in 1864, less than two decades after Texas had become a state. She was one of five children, and the second daughter of Mildred Emma Hoover and Aubrey "Bill" Murrill Cain.

My mother is a published author and began writing stories when she was 10-years old. In 1989, after my sister Courtney was born, my mother returned to writing in her spare time. Although, when I look back now I don't know how she had any spare time. She would go on to publish nine novels; a mixture of thrillers, suspense and even a mystery. It was after my youngest sister Megan started kindergarten that my mother returned to college. She attended the University of Texas at San Antonio and earned an undergraduate degree in English. She would then go on to receive a Master's in Education (Reading).

My father, Harvey Heber Brigham Fulmer, was born in 1940 in Des Moines, Iowa. He was the son of Frances Virginia Beverlin and Ervin Harvey Fulmer, a career U.S. Army Master Sergeant from Rock Island, Illinois. After his father passed away in Germany, my father, at the age of 13, returned to San Antonio with his mother. They had lived there years earlier when his father was stationed at what was then Kelly Field. Furthermore, my father's older brother John Fulmer was preparing to leave the U.S. Navy and return to San Antonio where his wife and children lived.

I've always thought that all great love stories begin with the couple meeting each other in an interesting way. My parents were no exception. They were high school sweethearts in the iconic 1950's at Luther Burbank High School on the south side of San Antonio. Although they attended the same high school they didn't meet until a school trip to El Paso in early January of 1956. They marched as part of the half-time show in the Sun Bowl between the Wyoming Cowboys and the Texas Tech Red Raiders. My father played the trombone and was first chair in the Bulldog Band. He was quiet but had lots of friends. He enjoyed swimming and listening to jazz and that other new form of music at the time called Rock-n-Roll. He was a good student and very confident. He once took the U.S. flag to the principal's office because it wasn't being folded correctly or handled respectfully. My mother was in the Orange Jackets, the Burbank High School pep squad. She was more outgoing than my dad. She has always described herself as a people-pleaser. She had many friends and loved playing tennis and going to parties. It was love at first sight for the outgoing southern belle and the quiet Yankee. They've been inseparable ever since, outstanding examples of love and devotion.

Growing up, my father working primarily in the advertising field. Money was tight, as was to be expected with such a large family. Occasionally, the electricity or water was turned off for half a day as my parents scrambled to find a way to pay the bill. Whenever our car broke down, which seemed to happen on a semi-regular basis, my father would perform the repairs himself. I recall holding a flashlight for him as he lay underneath the car late into the night making repairs. Like my mother, he possesses tenacity and an indefatigable work ethic. Still, we were often without a car and found ourselves getting rides to school, church or to the grocery store. My father sometimes worked two jobs to try to make ends meet. As a result, he was often gone for long hours.

I remember my mother once giving me a few dollar bills and asking me to buy a loaf of white bread, a small jar of Miracle Whip and a can of potted meat from the grocery store. At 10-years-old I would walk a mile to the Piggly Wiggly by myself, buy those few groceries and then walk the mile back home. Occasionally we had extra money and I could buy Chocolate Pinwheels. I remember seeing television commercials about Underwood Deviled Ham which looked a lot better to me than potted meat. I asked my mom about it one day wondering if we could perhaps, buy deviled ham instead of potted meat. But she said potted meat was cheaper. I never asked again. As the oldest, I grew accustomed to the way things were. The cupboards and refrigerator were often bare, with beans and rice and peanut butter and jelly sandwiches the common staples. We ate our fair share of peanut butter and jelly. By the time I left home at age 19 it would be another fifteen years or so before I could stand to eat another peanut butter and jelly sandwich. But like all parents my mother and father did the best they could. They both worked hard and we made do with what we had. No one starved. We all managed to somehow get enough to eat.

My mother was a very talented seamstress and would spend hours sewing cute clothes for my sisters and shirts for me before each school year. I also received hand-me-downs from extended family members but somehow the clothes never seemed to fit me just right. They were always from cousins who were much taller than I. On the other hand, I've never been accused of being a slave to fashion.

Although we had a large family we never lived in a house with more than three bedrooms. You can imagine how crowded that became. When I was 13 years old we moved to a house in Leon Valley, a small bedroom community on the sprawling northwest side of San Antonio. My parents would remain at this house until after I left for the U.S. Army in 1987. The home had a one-car garage that became my bedroom. Although it was wonderful to have the quiet and privacy of my own room, it was stifling hot in the summer and frequently ice-cold in the winter. That, plus having the washer and dryer unit running late into the evening made sleep difficult. The dryer exhaust emptied into the garage and added humidity to my already hot garage bedroom. Looking back now I have to laugh about it, but I remember I was embarrassed at the time to invite friends over because I didn't want them to know my bedroom was in the garage.

I may have had a modest upbringing, but I was happy. I understand there are those who would've been delighted to be so blessed. And maybe I'm making it sound worse than it was. We did have plenty of good times and everyone was healthy. We always had an abundance of love.

Aside from trips to the library and the movies, we spent time at the swimming pool each summer. I attended Boy Scout camp for four years at Bear Creek Scout Reservation, an idyllic camp in the Texas Hill Country near the city of Hunt. I returned for a fifth year and worked on staff as the quartermaster for Camp Friedrich. I played trumpet in the John Marshall High School Ram Band under the tutelage of the legendary band director, Charles L. Kuentz, Jr. My favorite part was performing during halftime at football games. We were also active in our church and visited relatives and friends. We took weekend trips out of town to state parks and landmarks. I had a paper route when I was younger and then worked as a short order cook when I was 16-years old at Swensen's Ice Cream and Fine Foods next to Ingram Park Mall. My parents instilled in me a sense of justice, a relationship with God and an egalitarian approach to life.

Shortly after my nineteenth birthday I left home and began serving a voluntary religious mission for The Church of Jesus Christ of Latter-Day Saints. For the next 18 months I served in the towns and mountains of western Montana and north central Wyoming and I had many wonderful and spiritual experiences. My mission inculcated within me dedication, an appreciation for hard work, and the virtues of planning and keeping to a schedule. These qualities would go on to help me when I became a private investigator.

I returned to San Antonio in the fall of 1984 uncertain of my future. I wanted to become a private investigator but was unsure about how to obtain the requisite experience I needed for the license. I wanted to attend college, but money was scarce. To be perfectly honest, I had always felt that a college education was reserved for people smarter than me. Or, at least for those with money. I had what motivational speaker Anthony Robbins called a "poor psychology." Up until this point in time, no one in my family had received a college degree. The task seemed Herculean. I didn't know how to go about it. I had no idea that loans, grants and scholarships were available to help students. Unlike many of my peers at Marshall High School, I had never focused on attending college. I made good marks in classes I enjoyed, such as history or band. But I didn't always apply myself in mathematics or science. Frankly, I didn't think any college would accept me.

After my church mission in Montana I also returned to my bedroom in the garage which I now shared with my oldest sister, Stacey. The garage was parted in the center by a couple of thick blankets strategically hung from the ceiling. This was not going to work. I often joked that with nine younger sisters, I never saw the inside of a bathroom until I was twenty-years old. And when I did, I had to negotiate an obstacle course of curling irons, hair straighteners and blow dryers. What I didn't want to do was go backwards to the way things were before I left. I had to make some changes. It was time to move on.

Around this time, Matthew Mozingo, a Mormon missionary I had served with in Montana, joined the U.S. Army to earn money for college. He had traveled from Logan, Utah to Fort Sam Houston in San Antonio for training and we spent some weekends together. My father had always regaled us with funny experiences he had in the military. I began to think that maybe the discipline, as well as the money they offered for college, made the Army an appealing option. Plus, I yearned to break out and travel. I had to get out of my parent's garage. On a warm July afternoon in 1987 I drove over to the military recruiter's office near Ingram Park Mall and joined the U.S. Army. I didn't know it at the time, but I was signing up for much more than I had bargained for.

CHAPTER 3

BROTHERS IN ARMS

Much like my family history in the criminal justice field, I also come from a long line of service members. My uncle George served in the Army and uncle Bubba retired from the U.S. Coast Guard. My father served both in the Marines and the Army during the Vietnam War. His father, Ervin Fulmer, served in both World War One and World War Two. By the time the Korean War rolled around in June of 1950, my grandfather had retired on disability. He had suffered a heart attack while at Kelly Field in San Antonio. However, like many World War Two veterans, he was called back into the service. But due to his disability, he was placed in a non-combat support role in Germany, serving first in Wiesbaden and later in Munich. He was a food service inspector for the U.S. Air Force mess facilities and traveled throughout Germany, France and England during that time.

Going back even further there were four Fulmer brothers who served with the 105th Pennsylvania Volunteer Infantry during the American Civil War. They fought at the battle of Gettysburg, and although wounded, miraculously, all four survived. One of them, John J. Fulmer, would go on to marry a young, pretty 24-year old immigrant named Sarah Louise Newham from the small village of Guilsborough, England. They married seven months after the Civil War ended. Sarah was my great, great grandmother.

And so, like my ancestors before me, I joined the service. I signed up for the Army on July 7, 1987 because I was bored. I signed up because I wanted to make a difference and because I wanted to get out of my parent's house and travel. But mostly because I needed money for college, to earn a degree in criminal justice. Like my forebear, John J. Fulmer, I signed up for the infantry for four years and qualified for the Montgomery G.I. Bill. At the young age of twenty-three I entered the San Antonio MEPS[xiii] and then flew to Atlanta, Georgia where I was placed on a bus with several other fresh recruits for the one hour and forty-five-minute drive to Ft. Benning, Georgia. I remained there from July until late September attending basic training, advanced infantry training and Army airborne school.

After my initial training had ended, I was staying overnight at a hotel in Columbus, Georgia with a couple of other soldiers. We would all fly out the next morning to our individual assignments. I was headed to Headquarters and Headquarters Company, 1st of the 502nd Infantry (First Strike); a unit of the storied 101st Airborne Division at Ft. Campbell, Kentucky. I was excited but also somewhat apprehensive about my first assignment. I hoped I would be up to the task. The hotel we stayed in was located on Victory Drive, or, as the local soldiers called it, the aptly named, "VD" drive.

Some ten minutes after checking in as we were getting situated in our room, we were surprised by a knock on the door. We all looked up at each other because we weren't expecting anyone. I opened the door to find an older soldier standing there in BDU's[xiv]. I could tell by his uniform that he was regularly stationed at Ft. Benning and that he was a Staff Sergeant. He smiled and said, "Hey fellows, do you need any girls?" I turned and looked at the guys who were with me and then back at the sergeant at the door. "I can get some girls over here," he said. By "girls," he meant prostitutes.

"Uh…no, we're fine." I said. "But thank you anyway." My polite thank you seemed suddenly out of place since we were talking about prostitutes. The sergeant obviously had a deal with the hotel clerk to alert him whenever soldiers had checked in. As I closed the door I couldn't believe an E-6 was pimping women. And in his Army uniform. That was my Army wake-up call.

At Ft. Benning, I was trained as an indirect fire infantryman (mortars). I would eventually go on to serve for the next four years with distinction earning numerous accolades, including the Combat Infantryman's Badge and the Southwest Asia Service Medal with two Bronze Stars. One was for the defense of Saudi Arabia and the other was for the liberation and defense of Kuwait. I served in the aforementioned 502nd Infantry and the equally famous 2nd Armored Division (Hell on Wheels) at Ft. Hood, Texas. It was while serving in the latter that my unit was called up to participate in the first Gulf War in 1990.

I would go on to spend a little over six months overseas in the deserts of Saudi Arabia and eventually move on to ground combat operations in Iraq. Prior to the escalation that led up to the Gulf War, the Army, in its infinite wisdom decided to deactivate my unit, the 2nd Squadron, 1st Cavalry Regiment (Blackhawks) of the 2nd Armored Division. General George S. Patton, "Old Blood and Guts" himself had commanded the division during World War Two. The unit had a rich history and played a celebrated role during combat operations. But evidently the rear echelon paper pushers at the Pentagon had no loyalty to the past; and no obvious appreciation for history or even an understanding of unit esprit de corps. And so, with the mere stroke of a pen they deactivated my division and shattered our morale in the process. I was sure General Patton was rolling over in his grave.

Shortly after my unit arrived in Saudi Arabia, our designation was therefore changed to 1st Squadron, 7th Cavalry (Garryowen),xv of the 1st Cavalry Division. This was the same unit that sustained heavy causalities in the 1965 Battle of Ia Drang Valley during the Vietnam War. That battle was the very first major conflict between U.S. forces and the North Vietnamese Army.xvi The 1/7 Cavalry was also General George Armstrong Custer's unit at the 1876 Battle of the Little Bighorn. They were all but decimated by Lakota, Cheyenne and other native American tribes under the command of Chief Sitting Bull. Unit history notwithstanding, I really hoped we had better luck in Iraq.

As it turns out, we did, although we saw brief combat action in the waning hours of the short 100-hour war. My particular unit was assigned as the scout element for the entire 1st Cavalry Division, a division that was originally one of several held in reserve by Allied Commander General Norman "Stormin' Norman" Schwarzkopf. However, due to the unexpectedly quick pace of the Allied advance, we ended up sweeping into Iraq as part of phase two. We were part of a large arc that cut off the Iraqi Army as they hastened a retreat from the tiny nation of Kuwait.

The morning the ground campaign started, my squad was in a forward support area getting our vehicle fixed. Our entire engine had been lifted out of our M113 Armored Personnel Carrierxvii (APC) and placed on the ground for repairs. Although I was in the middle of the desert in a war, I oddly spent that morning watching a movie. I watched the 1989 Tom Berenger film, *Major League* in a large Army tent with several other soldiers as I waited for my APC to be repaired. That afternoon my squad leader, Staff Sergeant David Onuschak, gathered us together and we took off through the desert to catch up with our unit.

As the tip of the spear for the entire 1st Cavalry Division, my unit breached the border of Saudi Arabia and Iraq, thus crossing the line of departure. Our mission was one of deception. Our maneuver was intended to fool the Iraqi Army into thinking that the major allied attack would come from near the Wadi Al-Batin.xviii   Gen. Schwarzkopf gave the order to the 1st Cavalry Division's commander, Major General John H. Tilelli, Jr., "Send in the First Team. Destroy the Republican Guard. Let's go home."

A day later, on February 27, 1990, we had refueled and moved a staggering 190 miles northeast into enemy territory. We had effectively cut off the way home for the Republican Guard.

On the second night of the war we ran headfirst into stragglers from the Nebuchadnezzar Division, a unit of the elite Republican Guard retreating from their pillaging of Kuwait. It was late at night and we were set up in a defensive posture when I suddenly heard the loud booming rat-a-tat-tat of the twenty-five-millimeter guns on several of our unit's Bradley Fighting Vehicles. They had fired on a BMP-1, a Russian Infantry Fighting Vehicle used by the Republican Guard that had wandered into our area. Unfortunately, my APC was in the middle of this crossfire. It was shortly after midnight, but I could see the brilliant piercing red tracers flying overhead as I hunkered down next to our 106-millimeter track-mounted mortar. The air was thick with the smell of cordite. The rear ramp of the APC was down, like a large mouth facing the dark unknown. I removed my .45 caliber Colt handgun from its leather shoulder holster and pointed it into the darkness, preparing for the unexpected. My adrenal glands were on fire, raw fear surging through my veins. My thoughts, as always, were on my family and whether I would ever see them again.

During the attack that night, several incoming rounds from an enemy mortar landed directly in front of my vehicle and shook the ground like a tremendous earthquake. I could hear the shrill whistling as the mortar rounds descended in my general direction; a sound I will not soon forget. It was especially frightening because I had no idea where the rounds would hit.

Several members of my squad, including SSG Onuschak, were absent. They had chosen this time to be off visiting another group of men in the unit. Left with only remnants of my mortar team and no instructions, I took the initiative. I sent a soldier out to set up aiming stakes, so we could prepare to fire our mortar, should it become necessary. My biggest fear was a direct hit to the APC. It was stocked full of white phosphorus and high explosive rounds as well as incendiary grenades that burned at 4,000 degrees Fahrenheit. If that had happened they would have needed tweezers to pick up what would have been left of me.

We succeeded in destroying the Iraqi units that night and killing the entire enemy crew. Before the war I had always wondered how I would react when the time came. I remember reading Stephen Crane's classic American novel *The Red Badge of Courage* as a child. Would I be brave? Would I be frozen with fear like Henry Fleming, the novel's young protagonist? Would the men be able to count on me? That night my reaction was a combination of all three. I had never experienced the degree of raw and unmitigated fear in my life as I did during the war. But when the time came…when it counted, I found that I could be counted upon. I remembered my training and did my job. I performed like a well-oiled machine. I attribute that to Sergeant First Class Theodore Slaughter, my former squad leader in the 101st Airborne Division. He was the ultimate warrior-philosopher, often singing the Irish folk songs of the Clancy Brothers as he trained us how to be good soldiers.

My platoon did not suffer any casualties during the war. However, there would be two deaths that would catch me off guard. About two weeks before my unit was activated for the war, a fellow I knew from the squadron got out of the Army early and returned to his home in California. He was a nice guy and I had spoken to him on many occasions. After the war started we all agreed he had been lucky to get out in what we saw as the nick of time. However, after we had been in Saudi Arabia for a couple of months we got word he had been killed in California in an automobile accident. I was stunned by the news. I had gone to war and he had gone home and died. It didn't seem fair. The news reached me at a time when I was paralyzed by fear. It made me realize that life is fragile and that when your number is up it doesn't matter where you are or what you're doing.

The other death involved Specialist Tracy. He was one of the mortar soldiers in my platoon. He was a quiet, shy African-American soldier that seemed to get along well with everyone. Once we moved out into the desert of Saudi Arabia however, he was overcome with fear. So much so that it was painfully obvious, and it began to affect the morale of the rest of the platoon. When a request came down from division to send one volunteer from our unit to King Khalid Military City (KKMC) to work an extended detail, Tracy was only too glad to volunteer. To be honest, we were all glad he was chosen. Fear, especially in a cohesive military unit, can be contagious. It can lead to mistakes. And mistakes can lead to casualties.

After the war was over and about a week before we returned home, Tracy quietly returned from KKMC and rejoined our platoon. He had survived the war by working an Army detail in an air-conditioned office safely in the rear. There was a bit of grumbling about his presence. There was a feeling that we had collectively suffered and had gone through our own unique ordeal while he hadn't been a part of our shared experience. Because of this, there was an underlying but fair amount of contempt for him by the rest of the platoon. I didn't give it too much thought because I knew the truth, that given half the chance, each of us would have traded places with him if we could. We were all just as afraid as he was. He did what we all deep down wanted to do. But we hated him for it. Because he reminded us of our own fears.

It wouldn't be until many years after I left the army that I learned he had eventually transferred to the 173 Airborne Brigade Combat Team (Sky Soldiers) in Vicenza, Italy where he lost his life in a parachuting accident. His parachute malfunctioned during a routine training exercise. It was further testimony to me that when the good Lord wants you home, he will take you.

Several days after the war ended I boarded a grey Marine Corp Sikorsky RH-53D Sea Stallion helicopter from somewhere in the middle of the desert in Iraq and flew into Kuwait. As we flew over downtown Kuwait City I could see the damaged buildings, burned out vehicles and the destruction left behind by the retreating Iraqi Republican Guard. I was only overseas for half a year, but it felt like a lifetime. After the air campaign started, but prior to the ground campaign commencing, I remember lying awake at night listening to the BBC on the radio and looking up at the millions of stars in the sky. I could feel the warm desert breeze on my face. With no illumination from any large cities nearby, the night sky in the desert was wide and expansive and the stars twinkled with the notion that anything was possible. It was breathtakingly beautiful. Peaceful. That is, until I heard the steady and unrelenting drone of the B-52's as they flew over my location heading for the Iraqi defensive positions only a stone's throw away. The U.S. Air Force pounded the absolute living daylights out of the enemy. There were times when I almost felt sorry for the poorly-trained and conscripted Iraqi soldiers. I am sure they were as scared as I was and only wanted to go home to their loved ones. But, as von Clausewitz said, "War is the continuation of politics by other means."[xix] So, there we were, facing each other in combat.

During the war, my mortar crew and I slept in and around our APC. The vehicle weighed twelve tons but every time the air force dropped bombs near us it would shake and vibrate the entire vehicle. There were times when I wondered if I would ever make it back home to the world as we called it. Rumors were swirling that my unit might remain in the Middle East for up to a year after the war. This concerned me because prior to the war I had been all set to get out of the Army in five months. I was going to begin college and fulfill my dream of becoming a private investigator. Once again, my future was uncertain. I had read the fine print when I volunteered. I knew the Army could and would extend my enlistment due to the war if necessary. This was something my grandfather Ervin Fulmer and many other World War Two veterans from the Greatest Generation discovered. Once the Korean War started they were called back into the service. For me, the not knowing was the hardest part. Not having a firm date as to when I would go home made my time overseas seem like an eternity. In fact, in true Army fashion, I didn't find out exactly when I would be leaving for home until forty-eight hours before I actually flew out.

Almost four hundred Americans would lose their lives in the Gulf War, and thousands more in the Iraq War that began thirteen years later. I would make my way back to Ft. Hood physically unscathed, though I did have several intense nightmares about the war for the first several months. They would often jar me out of a deep sleep in the middle of the night and I would suddenly sit up in bed sweating and breathing rapidly. The nightmares persisted for several months and eventually became worrisome to me. As a child I remember adults around me disparaging the Psychology vocation and accordingly, I had adopted the same pernicious attitude. I'm sure their approach coincided with the rise of popular Psychology in the 1960's and 1970's, much of which could be categorized as touchy-feely, feel-good fluff. It also didn't help that I was in the infantry. Professional soldiers, at least at that time, rarely admitted to challenges of the mental health persuasion. It would not be until my new bride urged me to get help that I finally made an appointment to speak to an Army psychologist. I sat down with him at Darnall Army Medical Center at Ft. Hood several months after the war and described what I had been going through. He said that I shouldn't be too concerned and that the nightmares would eventually go away. And he was right. They finally did.

I don't believe my experience in the war affected me much in the long run despite the death and destruction I witnessed. At least that's what I thought.

About five years later I was watching the movie *Courage Under Fire*. The movie chronicles events during the Gulf War and starred Denzel Washington, Meg Ryan, Lou Diamond Phillips and a then, little-known actor named Matt Damon. I remember sitting in the back row of the cool, darkened theater by myself. I watched the opening scenes that took place during the first hours of the Gulf War as the ground offensive began. Suddenly, all the memories, sounds and smells of the war immediately flooded into my consciousness. It was as if I had been transported back to Iraq in 1991. I silently began to weep. I cried uncontrollably for the first ten minutes of the film. I was surprised by how much it still affected me, even after all those years.

After returning from my service in the Middle East, I found myself a decorated combat veteran ready to leave the Army and start college. About eight months prior to my deployment to Saudi Arabia I began writing letters to a beautiful blue-eyed, twenty-year-old young woman from Spokane, Washington. Valerie had a gorgeous figure with long, slender legs and soft, shoulder-length brunette hair. She was six years younger than I and happened to be the college roommate of my sister, Jennifer. I first saw her picture in Jennifer's photo album on Christmas break in 1989 and was immediately struck by her beauty.

A few weeks later in January of 1990 I found myself in the middle of a lush, storybook snow-covered forest in southern Germany, somewhere between the cities of Nuremburg and Augsburg. I was there with the Army participating in what would turn out to be one of the last NATOxx Reforgerxxi military exercises, when I decided to write Valerie a letter out of the blue. And with that, we began corresponding.

Valerie had a calm demeanor and was a great listener. She possessed the capacity to somehow overlook my many flaws, and she laughed at my jokes. A warm friendship developed from our letter writing. After I returned from my deployment to Germany, I decided to take a couple of weeks leave and meet her. Jennifer accompanied me as I drove my dilapidated Toyota Corolla from Fort Hood in Killeen, Texas all the way to Rexburg, Idaho where Valerie was attending Ricks College[xxii]. I was standing on the second floor of an apartment balcony with my sister when I first saw Valerie and another friend approaching on foot. I had butterflies in my stomach. My mouth was dry as she walked up the stairs, but I tried to play it cool. I remember it as if it was yesterday. Like my parent's chance meeting in El Paso so many years ago, it was love at first sight, at least for me. She was even more stunning in person than I could have possibly imagined. She was thin and stood a couple of inches shorter than me. She had a warm splash of freckles across the bridge of her nose and a supreme gentleness that instinctively set me and others at ease. The whole experience, indeed, the entire two weeks I was there, was intense and magical; like catching lighting in a bottle. We talked for hours. I wanted to immediately know everything about her and she felt the same way about me. She skipped her college classes and we became inseparable during my short visit. I didn't want the two weeks to end. I even extended my leave two more days because I didn't want to leave Idaho.

Within just a few days of meeting her I knew she would be my wife. We were in the student center on campus playing air hockey when I looked up at her and I just knew. I instinctively understood that there would never be anyone else.

There couldn't be. And there never has been. I wanted to ask her to marry me but after a two-week whirlwind fairytale romance it seemed so sudden.

After my two weeks in Idaho, I returned to Ft. Hood and was consumed by thoughts of Valerie day and night. I brought her up in every conversation; even with strangers. I found it difficult to concentrate on my work. I just wanted to be with her. Seven days after I returned from Idaho I called her on a Sunday evening and asked her to marry me. I hated doing it over the telephone, but I had no choice. It had been three weeks since we had first met, and she said yes.

Fast forward six months after that and Valerie and her family drove straight through the night from Spokane to Dallas, Texas for our wedding. I had called her father, Michael Kraft, and asked for his permission to marry her, but had yet to meet him or the rest of the family until the day we married. Although my unit was already on high alert by that time, preparing to deploy to the Middle East, my First Sergeant graciously allowed me one day off to get married. Valerie and I were married in the Mormon Temple in north Dallas on a very hot and humid August morning. Due to my alert status, we didn't have the luxury of a honeymoon. Instead, after getting married we walked into McDonalds for lunch, me in my Army class A uniform and she in her wedding dress. We then drove the three hours back to Ft. Hood that afternoon and began our life together. That next morning, I went back to work preparing for war and Valerie prepared to be an Army wife. Four weeks later I climbed a set of air stairs and boarded an airplane at Robert Gray Army Airfield at Ft. Hood and headed off to war, not knowing if I would ever return. After a brief stop in England and then Italy, we landed twenty-one hours later in the port city of Dhahran, Saudi Arabia on the Arabian Gulf. And that was my young bride's introduction to the U.S. Army.

Now that I was back from the Gulf War I received an honorable discharge and left the service. I had given some serious thought about making the military a career, perhaps changing my MOSxxiii to military police and eventually CIDxxiv. I liked the discipline and the order it brought to my life. But I also wanted to go to college, something that didn't work well being an active duty infantry soldier. So, in July of 1991, Valerie and I moved from our small furnished one-bedroom apartment on Lake Road in Killeen, to San Antonio, Texas where I had been raised. I began using my G.I. Bill at San Antonio College and later at the University of Texas at San Antonio (UTSA). At the latter, I received a Bachelor of Arts degree in criminal justice with an emphasis in security management in August of 1998.

I would fulfill my dream of becoming a licensed private investigator while I was still attending UTSA. I happened to be reading the career section of the *San Antonio Express-News* one day when I saw an advertisement for a private investigator job. The ad requested that interested parties send a resume. Although I had neither the required experience nor a resume I decided to apply, knowing I had nothing to lose if I was rejected. I sent a cover letter stating that, while I did not have any experience, I had not learned any bad investigative habits either. I was tabula rasa. I could be trained exactly how the company desired for maximum results. My letter must have been convincing. Several days later I received a telephone call in the afternoon from San Antonio private investigator Mike Farmer.

He called me in for an interview and then took a chance and hired me. And the rest, as they say, is history.

CHAPTER 4

ON THE JOB TRAINING

Mike was an exceptional private investigator. He was patient, conscientious and a stickler for details. If surveillance was an art form, Mike would be Picasso. During his off time, he was a competitive cyclist and brought that same dedication and hard work to the investigative field. He grew up in the small town of Hamilton, Montana in the beautiful Bitterroot Valley in the shadow of the Sapphire Mountains. After graduating with a degree in Anthropology from the University of Montana in nearby Missoula, he gravitated toward the warmer climate of Houston, Texas. Once there, he began working for Lucian Burke, an older, curmudgeonly private eye with investigative offices throughout Texas. Lucian eventually talked Mike into opening an office in San Antonio and that's where I began conducting workers' compensation and insurance defense surveillance. One of my very first surveillance jobs was an insurance defense case involving a man named Paul Skerritt, a small-town football fanatic with a low back injury.

It's been said that the top three religions in Texas are football, football and football. I can tell you that's not an exaggeration. Football dominates at every level. Texas has two professional football teams, including the Dallas Cowboys, who boast a record of eight trips to the Super Bowl and five wins. The college football rivalry between the University of Texas Longhorns and the Texas A&M Aggies is well known and has been going on since 1894xxv. But it all begins at the high school level. From the largest cities to the smallest towns, high school football dominates the state like no other sport. Such was the case in the small town of La Vernia, about thirty miles east of San Antonio. Population: about one thousand.

Paul's son Duke played tight end on the high school football team, the La Vernia Bears. Duke was very talented. To say that Paul was a proud father would be an understatement. He never missed a game. In fact, Paul was a bit obsessive about football. And that's saying a lot considering it was Texas. He had all the accoutrements of a football fan. He would be there at every game waving his foam finger and yelling "We're number one!" to everyone and to no one in particular. Initially, Duke was embarrassed by his father's antics but surprisingly, he became a big hit in the small town.

Paul had been involved in a car accident and was claiming, among other various injuries, a severe low back pain that didn't allow him to go to work or to do much of anything. I conducted an activity check, which is a short half day surveillance to determine whether additional surveillance was warranted. Paul didn't do much during the activity check. But I made some discreet neighborhood inquires and learned that Paul would be at Duke's Friday night football game. I made a note to be there myself.

I had no clue how enthusiastic about football Paul really was. But as I look back after almost thirty years in this business, very little surprises me anymore. Shortly after 5:00 PM that Friday I set up a surveillance position near Paul's house with my car facing the direction Paul would most likely depart the neighborhood. As it turned out, I didn't have to wait long. Shortly before 6:00 PM he emerged from his home and walked over to his car in the driveway. Some things must be seen to be believed. Paul was about five feet, eight inches tall and rather chunky, weighing about two hundred and fifty pounds. He was dressed in white shoes, white pants and a blue La Vernia Bears football jersey. The jersey bore number thirty-four, his son Duke's number. In the flat Texas sun, I could see his face was painted white and his hair was dyed bright blue. And of course, he brought along his foam finger. As he pulled out of the driveway I slipped in behind him and chuckled as we took off towards the high school football stadium.

Ordinarily, it can be difficult to follow someone on foot through a crowd. But considering how Paul was dressed, I had no difficulty keeping an eye on him as we walked through the packed football stadium. I ended up sitting about five rows behind him and slightly to his right. To everyone else, I was just one of several spectators with a video camera. However, anyone that bothered to look close enough would notice that my camera always seemed to be pointed towards Paul, not towards the field.

Once the game began Paul underwent a personality change; a metamorphosis, if you will. He began yelling and jumping up during almost every play. I'm not a doctor, but evidently the alleged pain from his low back injury came and went. I continued to shoot video from my position behind him. By the time it was over I had more than an hour of video on Paul. Paul walking up the stadium stairs. Paul walking down the stadium stairs. Paul walking sideways in the bleachers. Paul flailing and waving his arms. Paul bending over and jumping up and down. Even Paul doing the wave. Basically, Paul doing every physical activity possible that was outside the scope of his alleged back injury. All I could think about all night was I was being paid to sit at a football game, eat a hot dog and shoot video of a man with blue hair. You can't make this stuff up.

Insurance defense cases, like Paul's automobile accident, are very common. I would go on to conduct thousands of similar cases over the next three decades. Many claimants, like Paul, do their best to exaggerate their injuries for the express purpose of getting as much money as possible when the claim is settled. Add in sketchy attorneys, dishonest chiropractors and mendacious physicians and you have a real racket where about $7 billion a year is lost to fraud. As a private investigator, I work for the insurance company and conduct surveillance to determine the extent of the claimant's injuries. The goal is to conclude whether a claimant's daily activities are within the scope of their alleged injuries. My work allows the insurance company to arrive at a fair settlement. I don't adjudicate, recommend or pass judgement. I just gather the facts. I would learn that the truth was often gray. It's almost always somewhere in the middle. Many of these folks are legitimately injured. Just not to the extent they claim to be. Other cases I have worked involved workers' compensation fraud. Like the investigation of Ben Stockton, a city bus driver from Austin, Texas.

Ben lived in Green Mills, a housing subdivision in an older part of Austin, not far from The University of Texas. It was late summer and I was ensconced in my surveillance vehicle under the cool shade of a large Huisache tree that hung over the street. I had lowered the windows a couple of inches to allow a gentle breeze to permeate my van. I could hear the steady chorus of the male cicadas as they vibrated their tymbales to attract the female of the species. Someone was mowing their lawn a few houses down and I could smell the freshly cut grass. I sat there patiently waiting for my subject to do something.

Ben Stockton was a rather portly fellow out on a workers' compensation claim due to a severe back injury. He was only five feet tall but weighed close to three hundred pounds. I always found it ironic that so many of my claimants with back injuries also happened to be obese. Perhaps there was a connection. According to his physician, Stockton was in so much pain he could barely sit or stand for any length of time. He could not bend or pick up anything over ten pounds. Apparently, he was in really bad shape. So much so that he continued to miss his required weekly physical therapy appointments because he simply "didn't feel well." This, of course, sent a red flag to the claims adjuster handling his case. Hence, my presence near his home. I was there to ascertain whether or not Stockton's activities, like Paul Skerritt's, were in line with his alleged injuries.

I had been there for two days already and had watched Stockton's wife and children come and go. But so far there was no sign of him. In lieu of any direct evidence, private eyes often speculate as to the whereabouts of their subject or even convince themselves that the subject no longer lives at the address in question. It's not uncommon to sit for hours in front of the subject's house only to learn that you've been watching an empty house. Or the wrong house. But I had checked the license plates of the vehicles in the driveway and they all belonged to Stockton. I had the right house. And I was patient. The Irish writer John Connolly once wrote: "*We all have our routines…but they must have a purpose and provide an outcome that we can see and take some comfort from, or else they have no use at all. Without that, they are like the endless pacing's of a caged animal…*"[xxvi] I understood this quote to mean that sooner or later Stockton would have to come outside. And when he did, I would be ready.

I didn't catch a break until the third day of surveillance when I noticed something curious that, up to this point, had somehow escaped me. At approximately 10:00 am and then again at about 1:00 pm each day the front door would open and a large Airedale Terrier with a thick black and brown coat ran out into the front yard to take care of business. The dog walked around the yard, stopped at a random spot and then relieved himself. Afterwards he walked around a bit more and stretched his legs until the front door eventually cracked open again. Then his master, whom I assumed to be Stockton, whistled, and the dog returned inside to his cushy lair. I had seen the dog during the first two days of surveillance but failed to give him the attention due. I hadn't realized that he had come from inside the house. I assumed it was a neighbor's dog. Apparently, Stockton could do all of this without revealing his presence. This made my job even more difficult. That is, until the following day when the dog refused to come inside.

It was precisely 10:07 am the next morning when the same scenario played out as it had the previous days. The great beast was released, and he took care of business as usual, however, when Stockton whistled for him to come inside at the appropriate time, nothing happened. The animal continued to run and frolic in the front yard ignoring his master. I suddenly sensed that the advantage had shifted to me. I turned my video camera to the front door and zoomed in. I was a vengeful Captain Ahab waiting for my white whale to appear.

Silence. Nothing. I could feel the cool breeze on the back of my neck. A bead of sweat gently slid down the inside of my forearm. In the distance, I heard the faint beeping of a garbage truck backing up. The great hound continued to play and the front door remained ajar. I waited. His master whistled. Still nothing.

Surely the denouement was at hand! Suddenly Stockton's chubby face appeared and I hit the record button on my video camera. He carefully surveyed the street; his beady little eyes shifting to the left then to the right; looking but seeing nothing. He then stepped out into the front yard in his bare feet.

He was wearing faded brown cargo shorts and a white San Antonio Spurs t-shirt. He moved towards the animal but the dog, assuming Stockton wanted to play, ran to the other side of the yard. I continued shooting video and carefully documented what played out next. For the next ten minutes Stockton chased, ran, swerved, dipped, bent over, ran sideways and jumped. He did just about everything he could do to catch the dog. All the while displaying physical activity in direct contradiction to his alleged injury and physical limitations. There appeared to be nothing wrong with Stockton. This was further evidenced when he ran full tilt and finally picked up his fifty-pound dog and carried him back into his home.

I packed up my video camera, adjusted my car seat and dropped the transmission into drive. I slowly turned the steering wheel and left the neighborhood. I mentally checked Ben Stockton off my list. I had no shortage of insurance fraud cases. In fact, over thirty percent of workers' compensation claims are believed to contain some measure of fraud. Per the Coalition Against Insurance Fraud, people like Paul Skerritt and Ben Stockton cost the public approximately $80 billion dollars a year. And we wonder why insurance rates are so high. It was clear I had my work cut out for me. Maybe the next guy had a dog too?

Although both Paul and Ben's cases involved personal injury fraud and workers' compensation fraud, two distinct types of insurance fraud, they're good examples of what the insurance industry calls soft fraud or opportunity fraud. It occurs when an otherwise law-abiding person exaggerates what is typically a legitimate insurance claim. I have always found it ironic that people who typically would never litter or illegally park in a handicapped parking space, nevertheless don't mind stretching the truth in the hopes of getting a few extra dollars out of an insurance company. It's part of the "everybody does it" mentality. The truth is everybody doesn't do it. But everybody ends up paying for it. I would eventually find that much of my insurance fraud cases existed in these gray areas; a shadowy nexus between legitimate claims and blatant, outright fraud.

I soon began working for Mike Farmer about five to six days a week conducting surveillance around my college classes. I somehow found the time to study. My work schedule included weekends and most holidays. As a private investigator, I've worked every holiday except Christmas Day. I was typically in place by 6:00 AM and worked until late afternoon. My initial training lasted for about two weeks and consisted of a ride along with Stuart "Stu" Hall, Mike's senior and most experienced investigator. Stu was a nice guy. He was tall, thin and blonde and looked like a Hollywood leading man straight from central casting. Stu was originally from Kerrville, a small town on the banks of the Guadalupe River nestled in the Texas Hill Country, about an hour northwest of San Antonio. While Stu did his best to train me, those first couple of weeks were a bit of a blur. They basically consisted of me asking questions, taking notes and watching Stu as he conducted surveillance. Although Stu was an exceptional investigator, I soon discovered that surveillance is best learned by doing, by hands on, by practical application. Once I began working alone I realized that some things could only be learned the hard way. And by that, I mean, by making mistakes. And I made plenty of them.

In fact, during the first several months of surveillance I made just about every possible mistake in the book. I lost my subject constantly. I was burned[xxvii] several times. Once, as I moved from the driver's seat to the back seat I accidentally hit the car horn with my rear end. I had the police called on me because I was set up in a stationary surveillance position that seemed out of place. Neighbors walked out to my car and asked if they could help me. One of them even brought me an ice cold soft drink and said it was too hot to be out there doing what I was doing, whatever I was doing. I set up on the wrong address a few times and left my headlights on several times after daylight saving time had begun. In all, not my finest hour.

I once followed an elderly couple from a rural area south of San Antonio to a physical therapy appointment on the far north side of San Antonio. I miraculously did so without losing them in heavy traffic. I was proud of my efforts. That is, until they parked and got out of their vehicle. They immediately turned my way and smiled and waved. I almost waved back out of habit.

Another time I set up a surveillance position in a run-down apartment complex on Fredericksburg road. My subject was a member of the Hell's Angels, a one-percenter[xxviii] motorcycle club. I wasn't there for more than twenty minutes when I saw him come barreling out his front door. He was enormous; well over six feet tall and weighing about three hundred pounds. All of it muscle. He had a handgun in his right hand but was holding it down next to his leg as he walked my way. At first, I thought it was just a coincidence that he was walking in my direction. However, as I looked through the eye-piece of my video camera it became abundantly clear he was heading straight for me. I turned the engine over and slammed the transmission into drive. My tires squealed and laid tread as I got out of there as fast as I could. Clearly, this was not going well.

Fortunately, Mike was patient. He was a consummate professional and understood that there would be a learning curve with new investigators and that I would eventually improve. And he was right. I slowly got better. I began to learn from my mistakes. In time, I improved greatly. In fact, I eventually became so good at surveillance and so adept at catching my subject committing fraud that Mike began referring to my collective successes as the "Fulmer Luck." The Roman Philosopher Seneca stated, *"Luck is what happens when preparation meets opportunity."* Whatever it was, I had plenty of it. As in the case of Diego Ramirez, the healthy bar back.xxix

Diego had allegedly injured his back working as a bar back; pun intended. Although he was collecting a weekly workers' compensation check, there was a rumor he was still working. The whole idea behind workers' compensation is that the subject is being compensated while they recover from a work injury. The claims adjuster suspected Diego of continuing to work on the side. I decided to pretext Diego. I telephoned him and explained that I had been referred to him by a friend of a friend. I was having a private party and understood he was a bartender. Was he interested in the job? He said yes, then I added that I would need to see him in action behind the bar before I agreed to hire him. Of course, there was no party and I never intended to hire him. The entire reason for the phone call was to find out where he was working in violation of his workers' compensation status. He told me he would be working Friday night at Casa Rio, a well-known Mexican restaurant on the Riverwalk in downtown San Antonio. I said I'd stop by after 8:00 PM and meet him.

This would turn out to be the first time Valerie and I worked a case together. Friday came, and we headed downtown to the Riverwalk. The San Antonio River, or Paseo del Rio, slowly and lazily winds and meanders throughout the heart of downtown San Antonio one story below street level. The banks of both sides of the river are replete with tourist shops, fine restaurants, art galleries, smoky bars, loud dance clubs and expensive hotels. Fifty-foot Bald Cypress trees line either side of the river providing a large canopy of shade. The atmosphere is relaxed and festive. After the Alamo, the Riverwalk is the second most-visited tourist attraction in San Antonio. Over twelve million people visit the Riverwalk each year spending about two billion dollars. Numerous conferences and conventions are held each year at the major luxury hotels that are located on either side of the river.

Casa Rio is on the Riverwalk situated between Commerce Street and W. Market Street. They offer the very best in Tex-Mex cuisine and have been in business since 1945. The waiters wear crisp white linen napkins on their arms. They serve up platters of juicy sizzling steak fajitas and frozen lime margaritas in large cocktail glasses lined with zesty kosher salt. Mariachi's clad in traditional black Charro suitsxxx wander throughout the dining area playing the folk music of Mexico. All the restaurants on the Riverwalk offer dining al fresco with tables next to the banks of the river. Casa Rio is no exception.

Despite the humidity, a warm, gentle breeze flowed lazily from across the river. I could hear the water gently lapping against the side of the river bank and the low and steady hum of a motor as a Riverwalk boat slowly floated by. The small barge was filled with tourists cruising up and down the San Antonio River as the tour guide offered historical anecdotes. Other boats were outfitted with long banquet tables covered in white linen tablecloths as patrons dined on Tex-Mex favorites by candlelight. As Valerie and I arrived I could hear people talking, glasses clinking and smell the fresh aroma of flour tortillas and chopped spicy pico de gallo. I spotted Diego immediately. He was behind the bar and, despite the breeze, had already worked up a sweat in the Texas heat. I steered the hostess into seating us at a table with a commanding view of the back of the bar. With the Riverwalk being a tourist haven, just about every other table had a video camera on it. This was before the proliferation of smart phones and video apps. I had my video camera on the table sitting in plain view next to my plate of spicy Chicken Enchiladas Verdes. I carefully aimed it towards Diego's direction and began shooting video. With the camera doing all the work Valerie and I sat back and enjoyed our meal. Diego looked my way a few times and Valerie seemed to think that he was on to us. However, I had given him no reason to suspect me. I was just another tourist with a video camera enjoying my meal.

 I gathered about an hour of videotape as Diego continually bent over and carried heavy green plastic crates of clean glasses. He frequently bent down into a waist-high cooler behind the bar and continued to display physical activity well outside the scope of his alleged injury. And that was that. You might be surprised to learn that when it comes to investigative work there isn't always a smoking gun. Diego was working a physically demanding job while at the same time receiving a check for a workers' compensation injury. My video wasn't sexy, but it would do.

Once the claims adjuster saw my video she ordered Diego to submit to a physical checkup by a physician. The doctor viewed the video and examined Diego. He then released Diego to return to work. Case dismissed.

Since leaving the Army and starting college Valerie and I had three children. Brandon was our oldest, followed by Dylan and then our youngest and only daughter, Alyssa. Most of Valerie's time was spent tending to the children as I worked full-time and attended college full-time. It wasn't easy for either of us, especially Valerie. While Dylan was healthy, Brandon had been born with Asperger's Syndromexxxi, a neurobiological disorder now categorized as High-Functioning Autism. Alyssa was born with spina bifida; specifically, Tethered Cord Syndrome; Lipomyelomeningocele, a very rare birth defect that affects the spine and often has neurological consequences. She had her first surgery at three months old and seven additional surgeries before she turned twelve. We have been the recipients of many miracles when it came to Alyssa's health. It was recommended that she have that first surgery as an infant to release the spinal cord that had attached itself to the base of her spine. Of all the places in the world we could've been living at that time, we just happened to be in San Antonio, which is also where Dr. Sara J. Gaskill and Dr. Arthur E. Marlin happened to be practicing medicine. And, as it turns out, these two world-famous pediatric neurosurgeons actually wrote the leading medical textbook on how to conduct the very type of surgery Alyssa required. So, in early 1997, Valerie and I huddled together, scared and alone in a surgery waiting area as these two brilliant surgeons performed the delicate surgery on our little girl. A woman from the local spina bifida support group arrived to sit with us. It was the longest wait of my life.

I was left with the stark reality that two of my three children were born with rare birth defects, although I've never really cared for that term. I've often wondered if it had something to do with my possible exposure to chemical or nerve agents during the Gulf War. Of course, it was highly publicized that not only did Saddam Hussein possess weapons of mass destructionxxxii, one of the key reasons the U.S. entered the war, but that he used them against the Kurds and Iran. The latter is a proven fact. Still, I had to wonder. As the ground war progressed, my unit moved deep into northwestern Iraq near the Ar Rumaylah Oil Field. This was in January and February of 1991, coincidentally the exact same time the U.S. bombed Iraq's weapons plants and storage sites. Poisonous clouds allegedly floated across Iraq infecting thousands of U.S. troops, many of whom came down with a variety of symptoms eventually labeled Gulf War Syndrome. I remember being told to apply my MOPPxxxiii gear more times than I care to remember throughout January and February of 1991. Six years later two of my three children suffered from neurological birth defects. Still, my children have been and continue to be an absolute joy to me and make life worth living.

Many believe that Saddam did not have weapons of mass destruction. Maybe he did and maybe he didn't. Maybe it was just remnants of his campaign against the Kurds and the Iranians. I don't know. What I do know is that about 250,000 of the 697,000 military personnel who served during the 1991 conflict suffer from Gulf War Syndrome. And if more than a third of the soldiers involved in the war suffer from this illness, I wonder if maybe it affected me and subsequently Brandon and Alyssa.

all my investigative jobs included fine Tex-Mex cuisine and dinner on the
k with my sweetheart. Despite what you see on television, much of it is
mundane. At times, it's even boring. Surveillance requires an immense amount of
patience and mental focus. For example, I might toil for 16 hours straight staring
at my subject's front door, only to drive away with about two minutes of video as
the subject walks to and from his mailbox. But you must be ready for those two
minutes. It may only be two minutes, but sometimes it's enough.

CHAPTER 5

THE INVESTIGATOR'S APPRENTICE

It all began with Phyllis Williams, a tall older woman in her late sixties with short grey hair. She had a round face with pleasant features and could always be seen wearing the same white t-shirt and orange shorts as she diligently worked in her flower beds. Her husband had passed away years ago and she had never remarried. She spent the majority of her time working in her yard and taking a peculiar interest in what was happening on her residential street. While she saw herself as a responsible citizen, many in the neighborhood considered her intrusive activities as meddling in their private affairs. She spent hours maintaining her front yard to the point that not a single leaf or blade of grass was out of place. This gave Phyllis a superb vantage point with which to observe the comings and goings of her neighbors. She was known to snitch on them for minor violations of the city code and telephone the dog catcher about strays. No one dared park on their lawn or allow their grass to get too out of control. If they did, Phyllis was always there to remind them.

The use of snitches and informants is common in the private investigation industry. Phyllis may have been a busybody, but it was her snooping that put an end to the hubris and unbridled greed of Rosie and Cherry Jordan; the only mother and teenage daughter insurance fraud team I've ever come across.

As with many insurance defense cases, Rosie and Cherry were, at least initially, legitimately injured. But like many fraudsters, they began to milk their case; that is, they began to exaggerate their injuries and drag out their recovery time for the express purpose of obtaining as much money in the settlement as possible. Rosie and Cherry had been involved in a car accident. They were not at fault. They were hit by a utility truck from Dallas County. The utility company was paying their medical bills and made attempts to settle the claim, but Rosie refused. Despite her first name, her disposition was anything but rosy. She continually complained that both her and her poor daughter Cherry had been severely injured, maybe even permanently. Why, they were lucky to be alive! She wanted a new car. She wanted more money. She wanted a different doctor. She even complained about a loss of consortiumxxxiv, although her injuries were not that serious. Rosie's vocal grievances continued unabated for months. She called the claims adjuster weekly. In fact, she was so aggravating to deal with that the claims adjuster with the utility company actually begged Rosie to get an attorney so she would no longer have to deal with her directly. However, Rosie said "I'm not sharing my money with a blood-sucking lawyer!" In Rosie's mind, it was already her money.

The English theoretical physicist Stephen Hawking once said, *"It is a waste of time to be angry about my disability…People won't have time for you if you are always angry or complaining."* This was a lesson Rosie and Cherry should've taken to heart. As it turns out the person who didn't have time for their complaining was Phyllis, their nosey next-door neighbor.

Several years prior to the accident when Rosie first moved into the neighborhood in Arlington, Texas, she had said something that angered Phyllis. It was so long ago that Phyllis herself couldn't recall the exact details. But she remembered the feeling of being slighted by Rosie that day. And she held on to that feeling. She had caressed it and taken care of it. She nurtured it until it became a full-grown grudge. And she had been anticipating a chance at payback ever since. The opportunity presented itself when Rosie happened to mention the car accident to Phyllis and added "I'm going to take that utility company for every penny they've got!"

Phyllis had observed Rosie and her daughter and determined that their injuries were minor. She saw her opportunity to finally exact some revenge. And she seized the moment. She picked up her telephone, called the utility company and repeated verbatim what Rosie had just told her. The utility company called their insurance company. And the insurance company called me.

I began my investigation and quickly discovered what Phyllis had recognized. That despite the car accident both Rosie and her seventeen-year-old daughter Cherry were, by all accounts, in relatively good health. Their injuries were substantially exaggerated. I also discovered that Cherry was the star of her high school volleyball team and Rosie her biggest fan. I checked the website for Arlington High School where Cherry was a student and made a couple of telephone calls. In short order, I had a copy of the volleyball game schedule and discovered that Cherry's Lady Colts Varsity Volleyball team would be playing the Grand Prairie High School Gophers the following Friday. And of course, as in the case of Paul Skerritt, I would be in attendance with my video camera in hand.

I arrived at Arlington High School that Friday in time for the 6:30 p.m. game. I grabbed an ice-cold Dr. Pepper and a warm hot dog with plenty of spicy mustard and freshly chopped onions and made my way to the top of the bleachers. I found a nice cozy spot on the visitor's side. This afforded me the perfect view. I could shoot video of both Cherry in action on the floor and Rosie seated in the opposite bleachers. It seemed as if every other person in the stands had a video camera. So again, just like my surveillance of Diego Ramirez on the Riverwalk in San Antonio, I sat there, enjoyed my meal and shot video of Rosie and Cherry in front of everyone. I looked like just another proud parent with a video camera.

Although I had already obtained a little video of Rosie prior to the game, this was the first time I had laid eyes on Cherry. I was struck by how tall and thin she was. She had very long muscular legs and was probably just a couple of inches shy of six feet. She had the perfect body shape for volleyball. With her long, straight brunette hair tied in a ponytail with a white ribbon, she leapt up and let loose with a powerful jump serve. Next, Cherry crouched down and then sprang up quickly extending her lithe, toned arms and used her fingertips to set the ball for one of her teammates. I got that on video too. Best of all, Cherry absolutely slammed, and by that, I mean viciously clobbered, the opposing team with several incredibly brutal spikes. Each spike was accompanied by a very high-pitched blood-curdling grunt. The grunts reminded me of my days spent in bayonet training in the Army at the Infantry School at Ft. Benning. Every time Cherry did this the crowd went nuts. The cheers seemed to reverberate throughout the gymnasium every time Cherry did anything. This girl was talented. And I got it all on video.

Meanwhile, on the other side of the bleachers, I also kept an eye on Rosie. Every time Cherry did anything amazing, which was regularly, Rosie literally jumped up and down. She would also yell and wave her arms high above her head. She would then begin clapping and turn to face the crowd nodding her head up and down as if to say, that's my daughter! I spent the entire evening pointing my video camera from the floor to the bleachers; from Cherry in action an up to Rosie in action.

In the end, due to the video evidence I obtained, Rosie and Cherry didn't receive the huge financial windfall they were expecting. In fact, they were forced to resolve their claim and received a significantly smaller monetary settlement; one that was more in line with their injuries instead of their exaggerated claims. Rosie could also thank her prying neighbor Phyllis for the smaller settlement. It just goes to show; you never know who is listening. And you never know who to trust.

One of the things that initially drew me to this profession was that every day is different. I don't sit behind a desk. It's not an eight hour a day, five day a week job. That's never been my style. I have no idea what will happen next. I never know what to expect when I pick up the telephone. In real life, as in the movies, it often begins with a telephone call. Like the day I received a telephone call about missing tortillas.

The great tortilla caper involved the strange disappearance of thousands of dollars of Mexican food products from Caliente Sabroso Foods in Houston, Texas. The apparent theft centered around missing tortillas and taco shells. And bottles of salsa. And jalapeños. And I'm not talking about a couple of packages of flour tortillas and a single jar of salsa. I'm talking about over $20,000.00 worth of missing product.

Caliente Sabroso Foods is a major wholesale distributor of Mexican food products to restaurants and grocery stores throughout the southwestern United States. The company was founded in 1949 by the Raul Estrada family. They began producing tasty pork tamales and fresh flour tortillas in the kitchen of their modest home in the Magnolia Park neighborhood near the Houston ship channel. At first, they sold them to friends, neighbors and co-workers. But soon the business began to take off. Over time, it slowly grew into a multi-million-dollar business offering over thirty different types of products. Since 1977 they have operated from a manufacturing plant and a set of warehouses on the east side of Houston near the intersection of Federal Road and Interstate Highway 10. It was there, at one of their food production plants, that I met senior facility manager Rocky Sepulveda.

Rocky was a short Hispanic man barely five feet tall with short brown hair and a firm handshake. He wore cowboy boots, starched Levi's and a western style long sleeve shirt. On his head was a white industrial hair cover. He handed one to me which I hurriedly put on as he gave me a quick tour of their manufacturing plant.

As far as Rocky could figure, Caliente Sabroso was missing about two pallets of product a week. This amounted to about $3,000.00 worth of Mexican food per week. It was such a small amount that it had gone unnoticed for several weeks until it was finally recognized as an irregularity in a normal monthly audit. All told, he figured they were probably out about $10,000.00 worth of product. This was minimal considering the millions Caliente Sabroso made each year. But it also meant someone was stealing from the company. And Rocky wanted to put a stop to it.

We did a walkthrough of the warehouse and I talked to Rocky about his inventory controls and security measures. The warehouse in question had security cameras, however the cameras were outdated. Furthermore, I discovered major dead spots which the cameras could not observe. Moreover, the warehouse did not have an alarm system and their key control procedures were problematic. Given the size and resources of the company, this surprised me. Based on what Rocky told me I concluded that it was most likely an inside job. Someone had probably made an extra key and was returning later in the evening after the warehouse was closed to load up on product. I left Rocky and returned to the office to prepare myself for what would be a late-night surveillance. I began charging my camera batteries and packing the equipment I would need for the surveillance.

The warehouse closed each night about 9:00 pm, depending on when the last truck departed. I grabbed an ice-cold Dr. Pepper, propped my feet up on my desk and tried to get into the mind of the person or persons who were helping themselves to the inventory. I figured the employee or employees were returning a couple of hours later to engage in their pilferage. Like Jupiter Jones of *The Three Investigators* book series, I believe in Occam's Razor[xxxv], the scientific theory suggesting that, given competing explanations for a problem, the simplest explanation is usually the most likely. If Caliente Sabroso Foods was missing two pallets a week, then the culprits must be using a truck or a van to transport the product. They might even have their own storage facility somewhere. And no one steals that much Mexican food for their own use. The thieves were more than likely selling it for pennies on the dollar to some of the smaller mom and pop Mexican restaurants in the Houston area; restaurants that wouldn't ask any questions.

I began by conducting surveillance on random evenings and at different times. This went on for a week or two without any success. Unfortunately, that's the nature of surveillance. By week two I was getting impatient and so was Rocky.

Which is ironic considering that the same multi-million-dollar company that wouldn't spring for an alarm system or update their security cameras, didn't want to pay too much for a theft investigation either. Then it happened, plain as day. Except it happened at night.

It was on a Wednesday evening in late November, shortly before midnight. The warehouse had been closed for a little over three hours. There was a full moon and a cool breeze flowing in from Trinity Bay. A light fog had also slowly begun to creep in. It was deathly quiet. The only sound I could hear was that of an occasional car driving by on a nearby road.

I had strategically positioned myself in an empty building across the alley from the Caliente Sabroso warehouse. I had moved back away from the large window and into the dark shadows when I saw him. I instantly felt my muscles tense up as a lone, male figure suddenly appeared through the fog and began walking in my direction. I rubbed my eyes and looked again. It wasn't an apparition. He walked quietly towards the warehouse, ascended the stairs next to the main loading dock and came to a stop at the warehouse door. He then turned and looked right at me. I think my heart skipped a beat. But he couldn't see me. Next, he looked up and down the road and then turned back to the door. I could see him remove a set of keys from his pocket. A beam of moonlight sliced through the fog and reflected on the metal keys as he inserted one into the door lock. I grabbed my cell phone and quickly punched re-dial. This was before cell phones offered texting capabilities. Somewhere, locked deep inside that warehouse, another of Mike Farmer's investigators, Mario Salazar, was hidden. Mario immediately answered his phone.

"One guy." I said. "He's coming in right now."

He quickly whispered, "Got it" and hung up. Mario remained in the warehouse for the next thirty minutes and, from his hidden perch, shot video of the plunderer as he slithered around hugging the walls to avoid the security cameras. Unbelievably, the culprit could somehow navigate a forklift without appearing on the security footage.

While Mario was dealing with the thief on the inside I suddenly noticed a set of oncoming headlights cutting through the fog at the far end of the alley. They seemed disembodied at first, as if they were floating in the mist. Then they abruptly turned down the alleyway and proceeded in my direction. Eventually I could make out the shape of a vehicle. It turned out to be a small orange and white U-Haul cargo truck driven by what I assumed was an accomplice. I could hear the tires splashing through puddles of water that had gathered from a cold rain earlier that evening. The U-Haul cruised slowly through the parking area and the brakes let out a long high-pitched squeak as the driver came to a slow halt in front of the loading dock. The driver extinguished the headlights and I could hear a loud metallic clunk as he shifted the transmission into reverse. He then turned the wheel in a wide arc and backed up the vehicle perfectly in front of the loading ramp. The driver climbed down from the cab and walked to the back of the truck where he jumped up on the rear bumper. Although I could no longer see him, I could hear the familiar rattle as he raised the rear cargo door of the U-Haul.

Meanwhile, bandit number one had already opened the warehouse door from the inside. Both myself and Mario were recording all this activity on video, including close-ups of the bandits' faces. I heard the familiar low hum of the fork lift and watched as bandit number one loaded two full pallets of Mexican food product into the back of the U-Haul with ease. He then locked up and both men got in the truck and departed. I ran out to my car and followed them, being careful to keep a healthy distance behind them. I tracked them to a residential neighborhood that, surprisingly, was less than a couple of miles away from the warehouse. They stopped in front of a random home. I obtained video of the passenger as he exited and waved goodnight including a close-up as he stood underneath his front porch light. The driver then continued to his home where I shot additional video of him as he parked the U-Haul in front of his house. I noted the home addresses of both men and then drove back and picked up Mario. We drove to a 24-hour Whataburger restaurant around the corner and compared notes.

The same scenario played out again on the following Wednesday shortly after midnight. These guys had no creativity. On the Wednesday after that they were back. But this time the company was ready. The bandits were busted in mid-thievery by detectives and police officers from the Houston Police Department who jumped out with guns drawn.

Like many companies, Caliente Sabroso Foods wanted to avoid any negative publicity, so the incident wasn't on the news or in the papers. And of course, my role in the investigation was entirely confidential. As it turns out, I was right, both bandits were current employees. They were well-liked, and one was even a shift supervisor who had a key to the warehouse. And as I predicted, they were selling the food products to local mom and pop Mexican restaurants in the Houston area for pennies on the dollar. Since they were stealing the product there was no cost to them. It was all profit. In the end it turned out to be about $20,000.00 worth of missing product, double what Rocky had originally suspected.

The plan had been hatched when the supervisor was eating a baloney sandwich on his break and stewing over everything that was wrong in his life. He looked up and happened to notice that the closed-circuit security cameras didn't seem to cover the entire warehouse. Furthermore, they were cheap, older cameras that didn't possess low light capabilities. A little more snooping around and he discovered the cameras were recording on a seven-day loop; meaning that every seven days the cameras began recording over the previous weeks footage. At the time, security camera systems still utilized VHS videotapes. With every consecutive seven days of recording over the previous week's video, the quality of the videotape became more and more degraded. Most companies, including Caliente Sabroso, failed to change the security videotapes with any frequency. In fact, one of the managers sheepishly admitted he couldn't recall the last time they had changed the tapes.

The supervisor's accomplice used the fork lift on Wednesdays during his regular shift to move two pallets to an area near the warehouse door and out of the view of the security cameras. No one ever questioned why. Once he arrived under the cover of darkness he could simply make his way quietly through the warehouse and load the pallets onto the truck without being seen by the security cameras. It was a foolproof plan. Or so they thought.

I wrapped up the final report and told Rocky that an updated security camera system with low light capabilities and an alarm system would more than likely have prevented the crime. I had barely finished my sentence when I noticed Rocky

ing his head. "The company doesn't want to spend that kind of said. Apparently when it came to shrinkage, $20,000.00 was an acceptable amount of loss. I shrugged my shoulders.

"You guys just lost twenty grand, maybe more, in stolen merchandise. And you still have the same problem. If you don't make changes, it's going to happen again."

I didn't realize it at the time, but my words would be prophetic. This wouldn't be the last time I investigated missing inventory for Caliente Sabroso Foods.

I made it through my first year as a private investigator and my skills eventually began to improve. While I didn't have an apprenticeship in the traditional sense, Mike was always there to explain investigative techniques. I always tried to learn something from my mistakes. Whenever I was burned or lost a subject I conducted a mental after-action report. I would pause and ask myself what I had done wrong and what I could do differently next time. When I'd arrived on a surveillance, I'd look at a map of the area and try to determine how the subject would most likely exit the neighborhood. I learned things don't necessarily happen in the private investigation field like they do on private detective television shows. Unlike on television and in the movies, it can sometimes be difficult to even recognize the subject. Often, I have a physical description but no photograph. Sometimes even a physical description isn't much help. I recall a case where the subject was a twenty-four-year-old white male whose height and weight were proportional. I pulled up next to his house only to watch five white males, all about twenty-four years old, get into five different cars and depart in fi directions. Who was I supposed to follow? Talk about a comedy of err(

There are times when a physical description does help. Like when my subject was a black female; four feet tall and weighing 300 pounds. I had no difficulty recognizing her when she stepped out of the house. However, most of the time on surveillance I am forced to rely on the subject's physical description and presence at the provided address. I also run the license plates of the vehicles at the residence to help me determine the subject's identity.

The advent of social media has made things easier. Everyone wants to share, post, like and connect. By searching social media I'm usually able to find pictures of the subject and learn a little about their lifestyle. I recall a case where I monitored the subject's Facebook page and discovered she was a member of a bowling league. With a little more snooping around I found out when and where the league met. I showed up the next night, grabbed a juicy cheeseburger and fries and sat down at a table with a commanding, elevated view of her lane. I shot video of her repeatedly lifting and bowling with a 12-pound ball. It was particularly good video, considering the fact that her alleged injury was her right hand and wrist; the same hand and wrist she was using to bowl. After that night, I was able to cross her off my list and move on to my next subject.

The nature of surveillance usually means hours of watching and waiting. However, there are those rare occasions when everything seems to come together. I once pulled up to my subject's house early on a Saturday morning and turned off the engine. I was enjoying a breakfast taco from Taco Cabana when I noticed a large white concrete mixer truck slowly driving down the road in my direction. The truck came to a halt in front of the subject's house and then backed up towards his driveway. My subject, Henry Graham walked out of his front door wearing a long sleeve light blue cotton shirt, Levi's and rubber work boots. He was accompanied by a couple of other men dressed in the same manner. I quickly put the taco down and picked up my video camera.

The truck driver jumped out of the cab and walked back to the rear of the truck where he began operating several hydraulic levers. He lowered the chute and then began pouring cement onto an area next to the driveway. Henry, who allegedly suffered from severe back pain, had apparently chosen today to widen his driveway. I was able to gather a lot of video. Henry used a bull float[xxxvi] to spread the cement evenly across his new driveway. Then he and the others got down on their knees and used trowels to finish the job.

The Fulmer Luck had struck again! It was exceedingly convenient to pull up to Henry's house and gather incriminating evidence almost immediately. Unfortunately, that was and is the exception and not the rule. The nature of surveillance is watching and waiting. Sometimes for hours. Sometimes for days. As private investigators, we often try to be more proactive. We frequently turn to other tools and methods to ensure success. The majority of private investigators pursue only legal methods. Unfortunately, some delve into the illegal ones.

CHAPTER 6

TRICKS OF THE TRADE

With cases like Diego Ramirez and Rosie and Cherry Jordan, using a video camera in plain view was perfect for the setting. That was over twenty years ago. Video camera technology has advanced considerably since that time. I currently use small state-of-the-art covert video cameras about the size of a thumb drive. They can record vibrant high definition color video for hours. With these new advanced covert cameras, I can gather video in just about any location. I can sit right next to my subject at a restaurant or bar and gather video without their knowledge. This is a marked improvement over the first generation of covert video cameras. They were bulky and unreliable, and rapidly consumed battery life.

One of the first such covert cameras I used was a wireless camera placed inside a large plastic San Antonio Spurs drinking mug. The accompanying battery unit was bulky and heavy and clipped to my belt underneath my shirt. The camera couldn't record video much longer than about thirty minutes. The video signal itself was sent wirelessly to a heavy, clumsy receiver I also wore on my belt. I first used it at a popular flea market on Austin Highway in northeast San Antonio.

My subject produced and sold her own jewelry at a booth inside the flea market. She was on workers' compensation from her regular day-time job for a hand injury but spent her weekends selling the jewelry. I gathered what I thought was some fairly good video of her sitting at her booth and using both hands. However, when I got back outside to my surveillance vehicle to view the video, I discovered the quality was very poor. The wireless signal had been frequently interrupted by some other electronic source. Whatever caused the interruption left my black and white video with a distorted view. Every ten seconds it would be fuzzy in much the same way a horizontal hold would malfunction on an old black and white television set. I was a bit dismayed. This kind of thing never seemed to happen on *Magnum, P.I.*

Along with covert video cameras, I began using pieces of equipment and other tricks of the trade to assist me in my investigations. Every investigation is different. And there are times when you're forced to be a little more creative. That's where the art of the pretext comes in. It was a skill I first learned and perfected while working for Mike Farmer.

For lack of a better explanation, a pretext is essentially a prank call. It can be done over the telephone or in person. It involves calling an individual and misrepresenting your identity with the express purpose of obtaining information pertinent to your investigation. Private investigators and law enforcement officers conduct pretexts. It's essentially undercover work. For example, you may telephone the subject's home under pretext to determine if the subject is present. Obviously, if the subject answers then you've confirmed the information and may continue surveillance. But, what if the subject's wife answers the telephone? In that instance, you simply represent yourself as Bob Smith with XYZ Company. You inform the subject's wife that you're conducting a job reference check on a new hire and her husband has been listed as a job reference. From this point, it's fairly simple to gather the information you are looking for, such as the subject's current whereabouts, when he'll be home, where he works, when is the best time to reach him at home, etc. I also utilized a special application that allows me to change my phone number. It has the ability to make my incoming number appear on caller ID as any specific phone number I want. This allows me to protect my identity. While pretexts are illegal in some states, such as California, I find them to be a useful and necessary investigative tool.

There are numerous types of pretexts suitable for just about any occasion. We used one back in the old days which, although not illegal; was at the very least unethical; primarily because it encouraged the subject to engage in behavior they otherwise might not engage in. It was utilized when we had been on surveillance for a couple of days and it became apparent the subject simply would not leave the house. We would call indicating we were with the local utility company. We would advise the subject that we had reports of a transformer on their street sparking and surging. We politely asked if they wouldn't mind walking outside to look up at it and see if it looked normal. If not, we would need to send out a repair crew. People like to be helpful. Most of the time they would do so. We would be sitting in a surveillance vehicle a couple of houses down and get a good look at the subject as he or she walked out. We finally had to stop using this particular pretext when one of our clients asked, "How come all your videos begin with the subject standing outside their house pointing up into the sky?"

One of the first pretexts I remember using involved a guy who simply would never leave his house. He lived in Fredericksburg, Texas and after four days of absolutely nothing to show for it, I was anxious for results. I called him up with a pretext stating I was a manager of the local grocery store. I congratulated him for winning our free grocery giveaway. Could he possibly come in and pick up his one-hundred-dollar grocery voucher sometime this week? He couldn't believe his luck. The subject was so excited I think he had already hung up the phone, jumped in his car and was a mile down the road before I had a chance to hang up my cell phone. I followed him to the grocery store and got excellent video of him smiling and practically running in. I prepared myself for what I was sure would be a significant change in his demeanor when he eventually walked back out. And I was right. A few minutes later he exited the store and stopped to look around. To say he looked unhappy was an understatement. He was downright angry. Obviously, the grocery store didn't know anything about a free one-hundred-dollar grocery giveaway. He kept looking left and right and out into the parking lot. He eventually went back home and never left his house again. Even though his insurance claim was obviously fraudulent, I still feel bad about that one.

Sometimes a pretext doesn't require an elaborate story. Sometimes it just involves a simple phone call. I had been trying to catch up with a guy named Jason Bell in San Antonio, but he worked construction jobs and never seemed to be around. I grew so frustrated I started knocking on his neighbors' doors telling them he was supposed to be selling me some nice tire rims, but I kept missing him. I spoke with a kind old lady two houses down who said she knew Jason. She said he was paving a parking lot for a convenience store at the intersection of Grissom Road and Tezel Road. I didn't ask her how she knew. I just jumped into my surveillance vehicle and took off for that intersection.

Ten minutes later I arrived at the convenience store and, sure enough, there was a construction crew laying down cement in the parking lot. There were seven workers. Two were Hispanic and the other five were white males. They were all dressed the same. Unfortunately, I didn't have a picture of Jason. He was obviously one of the five, but which one? I started to get perturbed again then I remembered I had Jason's cell phone number. I quickly positioned my vehicle with a clear view of the construction crew. I pulled up my video camera with my right hand and prepared to record. With my left hand, I dialed Jason's cell phone number. I then watched the crew. Suddenly, one of them pulled a cell phone out of his shirt pocket and I could hear Jason say "hello" on the other end. I smiled and quickly hung up the phone. I continued rolling video of Jason as he put his phone back in his pocket and then continued working. For the next couple of hours, I obtained excellent video of him spreading asphalt over the new parking lot.

While the pretext is a useful investigative tool, there are some stipulations. You cannot represent yourself as law enforcement or clergy. You cannot use it to obtain financial information. I no longer do any type of pretext that forces the subject to engage in a specific behavior. Once you go down that road it's a short route to roping the subject. Roping is when a private eye creates a specific predicament that forces the subject to engage in some type of physical activity. The investigator then documents the activity on video. With those early pretexts, all we did was ask the subject walk outdoors so they could be identified. The feeling was that if they were legitimately injured they would not do so. With roping, a private investigator follows a subject to a public location, such as a mall or a movie theater. Once the subject exits the vehicle and enters a business, the private eye then deflates one of the subject's tires. Later, when the subject returns to find his tire is flat he is forced to change it. The detective then documents all this physical activity on video. This is highly unethical, but you would be surprised how many private investigators still do it. Many of them carry small metal tire valve deflators with them. The pretexts I use involve gathering information or simply asking them their name.

Once I followed a woman I believed to be the subject from her house to the grocery store. She was a thirty-year-old white female with shoulder length blonde hair. She stood about five feet, eight inches tall and seemed to smile a lot. Unfortunately, she was with another woman who also fit the subject's description. I was confidant the first lady was my subject, but I had to be sure. I followed her into the grocery store to get her name, so I could identify her. I grabbed a shopping cart and quickly threw in a few items to make it appear I was shopping. I then slowly approached her down one of the aisles. Once I caught her eye, I pointed my finger at her. "Hey…I know you." I said. Understandably, she had a blank look on her face. I continued, "I think we went to the same high school." She continued looking at me, her brow furrowed as she tried to place a name with my face. "What is your name?" I asked.

"Rachel," she replied. Bingo. She was the subject. I quickly changed my approach.

"Oh, wow. I thought you were Tina Dockery," I continued. "I went to Clark High School with her. You look just like her." She mumbled something about how that was odd and then we went our separate ways. I ran out to my vehicle and waited for my newly identified subject to exit. Normally, I wouldn't allow a subject to see my face. However, in this case I didn't have much of a choice. I had to use this method to identify the subject.

Occasionally pretexts are required when you have very little information on the subject; which brings me to the mystery of the unknown golfer.

Someone once said that "...*to play golf was to spoil an otherwise enjoyable walk.*" I don't know if that's true. What I do know is that when you're receiving workers' compensation for allegedly injuring your back at work and you're out playing golf, then the last thing the fairway is going to be is fair. Such was the case of Fernando Sosa.

As is common in many investigations, I didn't know where Fernando lived. We had a couple of addresses, but they were both old addresses. His mail went to a post office box, which is an old dodge used by professional fraudsters. I had no idea what type of vehicle he drove. Frankly, I didn't know much of anything about Mr. Sosa. So much for the legendary clairvoyance of the hard-boiled private eye. Sometimes this happens because there's a disconnect between the claims adjuster and the private investigator. Claims handlers are overwhelmed with a multitude of cases. They occasionally fail to provide investigators with all the information they have. Such was the case with Fernando's claim. So, I pulled out my computer and logged into another tool in my investigative arsenal, the proprietary database.

With all due deference to the Sandra Bullock Movie, *The Net* and Kiefer Sutherland's television program, *24*, there is no single database for private investigators that will tell the whole story on a subject. At the most, you're gathering bits and pieces. As a private investigator, I utilize several proprietary databases the average person cannot access. The information in these databases is culled from credit headers[xxxvii], utility records, rental applications and other public and private sources. I can also run license plates, VIN[xxxviii] numbers, and conduct title checks of personal and commercial vehicles, watercraft and aircraft. Like a computer or a video camera, these databases are useful tools in the hands of a professional and ethical private investigator. Add the numerous public and government records available and social media websites, and it might surprise you how much information a private investigator can find. Much of what is found in a database still has to be confirmed the old-fashioned way; with shoe leather. In other words, by walking around, knocking on doors and asking questions. And that's exactly how I found Fernando's house right off Leopard Street in Corpus Christi, Texas.

The South Texas city of Corpus Christi was founded in 1839 as Kinney's Trading Post. This, "Sparkling City by the Sea," is a popular tourist destination and the eight largest city in Texas. The downtown area is nestled next to Corpus Christi Bay in the Western Gulf of Mexico and is the eight largest port in the U.S. It's home to the Texas State Aquarium and the U.S.S. Lexington, an Essex-Class aircraft carrier that saw action in the Pacific during World War Two. Nearby Padre Island National Sea Shore is the longest undeveloped barrier island in the world and a favorite beach destination for millions of tourists each year.

I set up surveillance on Fernando but after two days I hadn't had much success. I hadn't even seen anyone matching his description. There were several vehicles parked at the residence. I ran the license plates on each of them, but none were registered to the subject. As it turns out, they were all registered to individuals whose names I didn't recognize at addresses I hadn't heard of. That put a damper on my mood. Those issues aside, I also observed a nosey neighbor looking out her kitchen window at my surveillance vehicle. I figured it was just a matter of time before the police arrived and asked what I was doing parked in the neighborhood. Then, just like that, everything changed.

Two Hispanic men walked out to the driveway and began a conversation with each other. Based upon their age, height and approximate weight, either of them could have been Fernando. I've always thought that if my private investigation business didn't pan out I could always get a job guessing the age and weight of people at the circus. I had gone from no subject to having two possible subjects. Lesson number forty-two on surveillance: When in doubt – get video. It's always better to shoot video and find out later it wasn't your subject than to fail to obtain video and find out later it was. I shot video.

The two men stood in the driveway speaking when a teenager walked out carrying two golf bags. At the sight of the golf bags I sat up straight in my vehicle. This might be good, I thought. The teenager placed the bags in the trunk of a pale blue Chevrolet Lumina and then the two men split up. The first one returned inside the residence while the second got into the Chevy with the teenager. They backed out of the driveway and took off down the road. I hesitated for a moment. Should I stay with contestant number one at home or follow contestant number two? Many times, in my almost thirty years as a private investigator, I have been forced to make these types of snap decisions with less than complete information. With regards to the first guy, I could always come back to the house and start again. However, based on the golf bags I decided following contestant number two was the best course of action. Besides, it would be better to follow contestant number two and eventually rule him out as the subject, rather than to let him go only to find out later on that he was.

I followed the Chevy for what seemed like an eternity but was in reality only about thirty minutes. We ended up at Oso Beach Municipal Golf Course on South Alameda Street. As I followed him into the parking lot I felt an adrenaline surge. Fernando allegedly suffered from a back injury. If this turned out to be him, it was going to make for great video.

I got into position quickly and shot video as he pulled one of the golf bags out of the trunk and threw it over his left shoulder. Then he and the teenager made their way onto the course. Because I had not yet been able to determine whether he was my subject, I had to do something to identify him. Although it does happen from time to time, clients don't understand when you shoot video of the wrong person. The best way to prevent that from happening is to make every effort to identify the subject early on in the surveillance. I had to find out if this was Fernando. I watched as he and "little Fernando" carried their clubs and a green mesh bucket of white golf balls they had just purchased over to the driving range.

In the event that he turned out to be Fernando, I thought it best to shoot a little video of him on the driving range first. After all, once I approached him and learned he was the subject, I couldn't very well hang around. My presence would be too suspicious. Fortunately, there was a park bench directly behind his position at the shooting range. I got about thirty minutes of video on him. It was a continuous cycle of him bending over in hideous plaid pants and placing a small white Titleist golf ball on a tee. He then stood up, pulled his golf club up and to the right, and with tremendous force swung down and forward until I heard that familiar smack as the club struck the ball. I then watched the ball sail through the air almost out of sight. With his alleged back injury, hitting a golf ball is just about the worst thing you can do. It's all about bending and twisting the back.

After about a half hour of video I put away my covert camera and walked right up to him to initiate a pretext. It was actually simple. I just asked him what his name was.

"Excuse me, but are you Fernando Sosa?" I asked. He turned and looked at me. The moment of truth had arrived.

"Yeah," he said. "What's up?"

It was him. I'm not sure what I would've done if he had said no. "I was just up at the pro shop and apparently, there's a phone call for you." I said. "I guess it's important." This was years before cell phones were common. He thanked me and handed his golf club to little Fernando. As I turned around to leave I could hear him pull off the Velcro fastener on his leather golf glove as he prepared to remove the glove. He then started walking towards the pro shop. I quickly did an about face and got out of there as fast as I could. I spent the next hour shooting more video of him from my surveillance vehicle in the parking lot. According to his medical report Fernando Sosa was a rare and delicate flower. The good doctor obviously hadn't seen him on the driving range. He had a powerful golf swing.

Cases like Fernando Sosa's are common, so much so, that when it comes to insurance claims, there are numerous red flags alerting claims handlers to the possibility of fraud. One such indicator stipulates that subjects who are injured playing sports on the weekend often report to work the following Monday and blame the injury on a work-related accident which occurred that morning or the previous Friday. They do this to collect the workers' compensation benefits for what is essentially a non-work-related injury. Red flags such as these are just another tool investigators and claims adjusters use to identify fraud.

Besides covert cameras, pretexts and databases, another tool private investigators use are GPS trackers. GPS, or Global Positioning System trackers are very small devices about the size of a pager that emit an electronic signal about every minute to a cell phone network or a satellite orbiting the earth. The signal is then relayed back to a proprietary website and interfaced with a map in real-time. I have a computer tablet mounted in my surveillance vehicle and I can watch you drive from point A to point B on a map. I can tell if your car is idle or in motion. I can even see how fast you're driving. If I lose you in traffic I can simply consult my tracking software and immediately go to your location.

I use state-of-the-art, commercial-grade GPS trackers that I place in black, hard plastic, waterproof pelican cases. Each case has a 90-pound magnet that attaches to the underside of a car. Again, it's not as easy as it looks on television. I've learned there are some areas where the signal won't get through. Automobile manufacturers have begun using generous amounts of plastic and rubber in newer cars. It can be difficult to find an area to attach the tracker. The GPS tracker battery must also be recharged periodically. I use special extended thirty-day batteries so I don't' have to switch out the device more than about once a month. And I've only lost a tracker once, all because the subject washed her car.

It involved a nasty divorce case in Grand Junction, Colorado. I placed a GPS tracker underneath a blue Lincoln Navigator driven by the client's soon to be ex-wife, Stella Kaufmann. Everything was good for the first few weeks. She went about her business running errands and meeting her paramour on Tuesdays and

Fridays for some afternoon delight at a no-tell motel near the intersection of Horizon Drive and Interstate Highway 70. Everything was good, that is, until the signal ended up at a business park where it remained stationary throughout the weekend. The signal disappeared the following Monday morning. At first, I thought perhaps the battery had died. But I did a little snooping of my own and discovered the final address for my now missing-in-action tracker, was Stella's attorney's office.

I learned later from my client Trent Kaufmann, that his ex-wife had called and accused him of placing a tracker on her vehicle in an attempt to stalk her. He was honestly able to tell Stella that he had not placed the tracker on her vehicle. Apparently, she was very serious about having a clean car. She had taken it to a self-serve car wash where, in the middle of spraying her tires with Armor All and washing the inside of her fender wells, she happened to see the small black pelican case housing the GPS tracker. She didn't know much about cars, but the black device seemed out of place to her. She drove directly to her attorney's office who immediately recognized it for what it was. Of course, in every other case GPS trackers have been invaluable in locating and following the subject. But I had to grumble a bit over losing a three hundred and fifty-dollar GPS tracker.

When it comes to equipment like GPS trackers and other tricks of the trade used by private eyes, what you see on television and in the movies, is frequently inaccurate. Private investigators do use numerous types of gadgets, but the reality is our main tools consist of the telephone, camera and computer.

I continued to work for Mike Farmer throughout 1998. In August of that year I graduated from the UTSA with a Bachelor of Arts degree in criminal justice.

Now that I had a college degree I began to consider other employment options. I had learned a lot working for Mike Farmer but without any benefits and no real opportunity for advancement I never considered it a long-term career. Furthermore, I had three children under the age of five, two with special needs. Add to that a fresh heaping load of school loan debt and it certainly wasn't time to strike out on my own as a private eye. I needed a more stable solution which, at least in the meantime, would provide benefits for my family and add to my investigative experience. I would find it as a government contractor. I was given U.S. Government credentials and a badge. But first I had to travel to rural Pennsylvania where I was trained by government agents in a secret underground cave in the middle of nowhere.

CHAPTER 7

GEORGE BUSH AND THE SECRET GOVERNMENT CAVE

I felt like Batman. After being granted a top-secret security clearance by the U.S. government, I began my training 230 feet underground in a cave in rural western Pennsylvania. The government site was heavily fortified and guarded by security officers with automatic weapons. No, that's not the opening of a Robert Ludlum novel. That was my real life in January of 1999.

In Summer of 1998 my father mentioned a company called US Investigations Services was hiring. I had never heard of them. Nevertheless, I headed over to their local San Antonio location in a three-story office building near the intersection of Broadway and Loop 410 to fill out an application. When I discovered the woman who took my application was from Chicago, I spontaneously launched into Carl Sandburg's epic poem, *Chicago*; "...*Stormy, husky, brawling, City of the Big Shoulders*..."xxxix She got a kick out of it and I watched her place my application on the top of the stack. Whatever it takes, I suppose.

US Investigations Services was formed in 1996 when the U.S. Office of Personnel Management'sxl (OPM) investigative arm, the Office of Federal Investigations (OFI), was privatized. The move was due in part to then Vice President Al Gore's efforts to reduce the size of government regulation and bureaucracy. Up until this time OFI was responsible for conducting the majority of national security background investigations on government applicants as well as the periodic reinvestigationsxli of government employees who held security clearances. Typically, every government employee who holds a security clearance is reinvestigated every five years to ensure they are still eligible to hold the clearance. With privatization, US Investigations Services shortened their name to USIS and overnight, became an employee-owned business that conducted about two-thirds of OPM's background investigations.

It took about six months for USIS to complete their background investigation on me. I learned later they had lost my paperwork and that the normal turnaround time is less than three months. Interestingly, their recklessness with my paperwork would presage tragic events to come some fifteen years later. But for now, I was hired. I was eventually granted a top-secret security clearance by the U.S. government and instructed to fly to Butler, Pennsylvania, where I would begin my training.

I broke the news to Mike Farmer that I would be leaving. I was concerned about how he would take it. Insurance claims surveillance is very competitive and good investigators are hard to find. As it turned out my concerns were unfounded because he took it surprisingly well. In fact, he was very magnanimous. He was actually excited for me and my future. He graciously offered me a couple of weeks' severance pay and wished me luck in my new endeavors. He said he had expected as much once I had graduated from college. We ended up parting on decent terms, which is good because it would not be the last time I worked for Mike Farmer. Incidentally, years later Mike was giving an interview to a reporter with *The Mid-Missouri Business Journal*. The reporter was writing a news story on me. Mike described me as one of the best investigators he had ever worked with. I guess that about says it all.

Shortly after Christmas in 1998, I hopped a flight to Cleveland, Ohio and stepped out of Cleveland Hopkins International Airport into one of the coldest winters I've ever experienced. I could feel the frigid wind from Lake Erie on my face and I thought I was going to turn to ice. I took an airport shuttle to the car rental area where I quickly jumped into a warm rental car and raced down the highway towards Butler, Pennsylvania.

Butler is a small town of about 13,000 people a little over thirty miles north of Pittsburgh. It's set among rural Pennsylvania with breathtaking panoramic views of thick, beautiful forests, Christmas tree farms, and gentle rolling hills. The training lasted for about three weeks and, although I stayed each night at the Marriott Hotel in Butler along with the other trainees, I traveled 18 miles north each morning to a secret government site just west of Annandale, Pennsylvania. Once in Annandale, which was really nothing more than a general store and a post office, I turned left on Branchton Road, a winding rural highway surrounded by thick forests on both sides. About a mile down the road I came around a bend and saw a very strange sight. There, in a vast clearing off to the right of the highway, were several large parking lots completely full of cars. But there wasn't a building in sight. As it turned out, the government training I received was conducted several hundred feet underground in a heavily secured cave. And when I first got there they wouldn't even let me in.

The cave is an old limestone mine the U.S. government bought in 1958 to store government records. The climate underground is controlled naturally, and the temperature remains constant year-round. The cool air and low humidity helps preserve government documents in a perfect state. The Mines, as the locals call them, stretch several miles underground and are large enough to drive a couple of semi-trailer trucks through, side by side. The walls are all solid jagged whitewashed limestone. Every few yards you had what, for lack of a better word, could be referred to as a storefront. Some, like OPM and USIS, were clearly marked. Others were not. Several U.S. intelligence agencies supposedly stored records down there. The mine is rumored to be able to withstand a direct nuclear attack; yet another reason the government uses it to store records. I had no desire to find out if that that little nugget of trivia was true.

Both OPM and USIS maintain offices deep in the mine.xlii After parking my rental car, I joined the crowd of other employees and trainees and began walking down a long blue canvas-covered walkway that slowly descended from the parking lot down to the entrance of the mine. There were two separate security entrances with armed and uniformed security personnel carrying automatic weapons and checking everyone's identification. Although I had been hired and told to report to the cave for training, when I attempted to pass through security they had no record of me being in the training class. I stood there for about twenty minutes as the security officer made several telephone calls. Somehow the issue was eventually resolved and I entered the cave, turned right, and walked a hundred yards to the USIS storefront and opened the door to my new government career.

The initial training centered around the history of USIS and what a great company they were. But most of it involved OPM procedures and government processes as well as extensive training in taking statements and interviewing people. After my three weeks of training ended, I boarded a flight in Cleveland and flew to Dallas, Texas where I began working for USIS out of their Dallas district office. It was a small but highly secure office on the eighth floor of the Earle Cabell Federal Building downtown on Commerce Street. Entrance to the office was by means of video intercom. When I pressed the intercom, Gavin Kingston, the USIS secretary, could observe me standing in the corridor. He would then press a button to disengage the electric door lock. Once I heard the loud buzzer I turned the door knob and was allowed entry. Gavin was a slightly overweight, older gentleman with white hair. He was in his late sixties and was close to retirement, having worked for OPM, and now USIS, for almost thirty years.

For the first two to three weeks I worked all my cases with a senior trainer, Bill Moss. He had been a federal investigator with OFI prior to the privatization of government background investigations and the creation of USIS. Moss was a few inches shy of six feet with short brown hair and green eyes that seemed to notice everything. Despite his taciturn manner, he was a consummate professional and trained me well. We returned from lunch one day to find the federal building on lock down. The police were not allowing anyone in the building. Several police vehicles belonging to the Federal Protective Service (FPS)[xliii] were parked near the building entrance at odd angles as if they had arrived in a hurry. The Internal Revenue Service (IRS) maintained an office in the same building and apparently someone had left a paper sack in front of their office. The police were preparing to call in the bomb squad when some brave soul peaked in and discovered it was an employee's lunch.

For my investigative work OPM issued me a special, encrypted laptop computer which we referred to as a "GRiD.[xliv]" Despite being technologically out of date, the thing weighed a ton and was virtually indestructible. It was during my training that I first heard a story which has been retold so many times it has since become part of OPM lore. It involved a government investigator who had his car broken into. Everything was stolen, including his GRiD laptop computer. However, the police ultimately recovered his GRiD in a nearby dumpster. Evidently the thief thought it was garbage. The investigators I worked with found that hilarious, as it was something we could all certainly relate to. The GRiD computers were eventually replaced with new state-of-the-art Compass Presario laptops.

After my initial training with Bill Moss ended, I spent most of my time working throughout Ft. Worth and Arlington, Texas dealing with the Immigration and Naturalization Service (INS), Federal Bureau of Prisons (BOP), U.S. Attorney's Office and numerous other individuals at state and federal government agencies. Every day was an adventure.

I was once interviewing the regional director of the INS in his Dallas office, but I absolutely could not stay in my chair. He had a very expensive set of brown leather seats in his office. As I sat there interviewing him and writing notes on my small notepad I slowly began to slide forward and off the chair. No matter what I did I absolutely could not seem to stay on the chair. If the director noticed, he didn't say anything. He was very pleasant to me. He had gotten off subject and began talking about his recent vacation. While he sat there and droned on and on I finally had to plant my shoes firmly in the carpet and lock my knees to stay in the chair. I walked out of there wondering why the government was spending all that money on leather furniture. Maybe it was so the INS regional director didn't have to endure long interviews.

Not everyone I interviewed was amiable like the INS director. I was once doing a background investigation on a young man named Boone. He had applied for a position with the U.S. Marshal Service. He listed his uncle, Roy Booker as a reference. Roy was a Deputy U.S. Marshal in the Ft. Worth, Texas area. Evidently Boone was following in his uncle's footsteps. I called the number to set up an appointment and it turned out to be Roy's home telephone number. I spoke briefly with his wife. She was very gracious as she took a message from me. Not more than five minutes later I got a call from Roy Booker. I was excited to talk to a real U.S. Marshal. That is, until Roy began to denigrate me for deigning to call his home phone and speak to his wife. I explained who I was and that this was for his nephew Boone. He didn't care. He berated me up one side and down the other. I finally hung up on him when he suggested I do something to myself that was physically impossible.

After only six months working in the Dallas area, I got a call from Wanda Ashworth, the Dallas District manager for USIS. A fellow Texan, Wanda had been with OFI for decades before joining USIS in 1996. She was in her late sixties with shoulder length brown hair and a warm smile. She asked if I'd be interested in transferring. A very busy one-person duty station had opened in Huntsville, Texas and she thought I might be the right person to run it. I didn't particularly want to move again, but I was eager to do well and be flexible in my new job. So, despite our recent move from San Antonio to Arlington, Texas, we packed everything up again and moved to Huntsville.

Huntsville is a charming town of about 38,000 people nestled in the thick piney woods of East Texas. Situated off Interstate Highway 45, it lies mid-way between the cities of Dallas and Houston. Huntsville is home to the Texas Department of Criminal Justice (TDCJ) and there are about ten state prisons in and around town. It's also home to Sam Houston State University. We rented a large two-story house in the Avenues and I went back to conducting national security background investigations for the federal government. With Huntsville as my new home base, I traveled throughout east Texas conducting investigations at several colleges and universities such as Texas A&M University, Stephen F. Austin University, Sam Houston State University and Blinn College. Because much of my work involved the BOP, I spent a great deal of time at several federal and Texas state prisons in and around Huntsville. I also worked several investigations at the National Aeronautics and Space Administration's (NASA)xlv Lyndon B. Johnson Space Center in Houston. In terms of security, NASA and the Ft. Worth location of the Federal Bureau of Engraving and Printing had the tightest security I had ever seen or experienced.

One of my first major cases involved conducting the national security background checks on the staff of the George H. W. Bush Presidential Library and Museum. The Bush Library is in Research Park on the west campus of Texas A&M University in College Station, Texas. The 90-acre property, built at a cost of $43 million dollars, holds the museum, presidential library and two auditoriums, as well as the Annenberg Presidential Conference Center and the George Bush School of Government and Public Service. Additionally, there is a small second floor apartment directly behind the museum where President and Mrs. Bush stay when they are in town. While conducting investigations I also had an opportunity to tour the museum. I enjoyed the Gulf War exhibit since I am a veteran of that conflict.

The library holds the presidential collection of George H. W. Bush, the 41st president of the United States. The collection includes over 44 million papers and documents, two million photographs and thousands of other artifacts, videos and recordings. The library operates under the direction of the Presidential Libraries Act of 1955xlvi and the National Archives and Records Administration (NARA)xlvii.

At the time of my arrival the Bush Library was in a state of flux, having been open for less than two years. I was involved in conducting a background investigation on Spencer Winthrop, the new incoming director of the Bush Library as well as several of the NARA archivists. This was 1999, the final years of the Bill Clinton presidency. Several of the NARA archivists who would eventually move to Little Rock, Arkansas and staff the future Clinton Presidential Library were currently in training at the Bush Library. I conducted all of their periodic reinvestigations.

Although the library and museum were managed by NARA, there was clearly an overt atmosphere of politics involved. I spent a good deal of time there and often felt a sense of political pressure and heightened expectations regarding the outcome of my investigations. Although I felt it, I never gave in to it. I've never been one to play those kinds of games. Prior to conducting the interview for Winthrop's security clearance, Wanda Ashworth casually reminded me that, although Winthrop was technically a government employee with NARA, he also happened to be a close personal friend of the Bush family and had essentially been hand-picked by President Bush to be the next director of the museum and library. After saying this, she paused and allowed her words to hang in the air a bit.

Nothing more was said, but I got the message. I understood this to mean that I needed to conduct the investigation by the book and to practice some discretion; which was how I conducted every investigation, regardless of who the subject was.

As it turns out, Winthrop was extremely gracious and very easy to work with. He welcomed me into his office and reached into a small mini-refrigerator and offered me an ice-cold Dr. Pepper before the interview began. I hope he wasn't trying to bribe me. He was a graduate of Southern Methodist University in Dallas and all he wanted to talk about was their upcoming football game with their arch rivals, the TCU Horned Frogs. Several of the library's archivists were SMU graduates and they all were close friends as well as co-workers. The other museum employees referred to them as Smoothies, or the SMU Mafia. They all planned to get together and bar-b-que before the big game.

During that same time Steve Redd, a childhood friend of mine from San Antonio, was completing his Ph.D. in Political Science at the George Bush School of Government and Public Service. We often had lunch whenever I was in town. One afternoon, he and I had an opportunity to attend a conference broadcast by C-SPAN[xlviii] that was held in one of the auditoriums of the Bush Library. President Bush was in attendance and spoke briefly before leaving early. It was the first time I had been in the company of a U.S. president. Bush seemed a lot taller in person than on television. There also seemed to be an awful lot of unnecessary standing and clapping. I think if President Bush had sneezed everyone would have stood up and clapped. I was also able to meet a couple of the other speakers including Leon Panetta[xlix], former chief of staff to President Bill Clinton, and future CIA Director under President Barack Obama. Also, in attendance was Senator John Kasich[l], a

U.S. Representative from Ohio and chairman of the House Budget Committee. Kasich would go on to run for President of the United States in 2016. I would spend a great deal of time at Texas A&M conducting investigations, many of which involved security clearances granted through the U.S. Department of Energy (DOE)li.

In a quiet, wooded area not far from the Bush Presidential Library lies a small, one megawatt research nuclear reactorlii. Most folks in College Station have no idea a nuclear reactor sits in their back yard. The reactor, part of the nuclear engineering program at Texas A&M, is used to train students and to produce radioactive isotopes for research. It is located off the appropriately named, Nuclear Science Road not far from Easterwood Airport. In early 2000, I found myself conducting all of the national security background investigations for the nuclear engineering department, which included both students and faculty. Due to the classified nature of their work, most of the faculty possessed a specialized DOE security clearance referred to as a Q clearanceliii. Federal background investigations have specific requirements depending on the nature of the background and whether it is a new investigation or a periodic reinvestigation. The number of sources, or references, to be interviewed is precisely enumerated in the blue OPM binder I carried with me at all times. Sources must address specific time periods within the subject's life. All gaps in school and employment must be addressed. Sometimes, as in the case of Roy Phillips, who was a student applying for a Q clearance, sources are difficult to find. I ended up having to interview Roy's girlfriend Roxanne because she was the one person I found that could address a small period of self-employment he had prior to starting school at Texas

A&M. Additionally, she had been present when Roy was arrested for public intoxication outside the Dixie Chicken, a local college watering hole on University Drive in Bryan, Texas.

On the day of the interviews I met Roy and his girlfriend at their nondescript apartment not far from the university. Roy, who was originally from Stephenville, Texas, was graduating in less than a month with a degree in nuclear engineering and had applied for a position with the DOE. He met me at his apartment door with a firm handshake that would take the rust off a door knob. Roy didn't look like a nuclear engineering student. He was a tall, lanky cowboy wearing a long sleeve western shirt buttoned all the way to the top and faded starched Levi's. He was quiet and reserved and peppered his replies with "yes sir" and "no sir." He looked and sounded a lot like the Marlboro Man. Roxanne was just the opposite; a short, bubbly blond wearing a baby blue tank top that barely covered her breasts and a short beige mini-skirt. She also didn't appear to be wearing a bra. I didn't give it much thought at the time. After all, it was May and already very hot and humid in College Station. But after what transpired later it all began to make sense.

Normally, I would interview Roy first. But I decided to interview Roxanne first because she had been present during the public intoxication arrest and I wanted to hear her version before asking Roy about his. Roy excused himself and quietly lumbered up the carpeted stairs to the second floor of their apartment as Roxanne motioned me to a chair positioned at the end of their couch. I could hear the creaking of the stairs as the sound of Roy's footsteps eventually faded. Once I heard an upstairs door close, I sat down and presented Roxanne with my government credentials. She sat down on the couch directly to my right. As she did so the hemline on her mini-skirt rose to mid-thigh revealing a pair of firm thighs and tan legs.

Part of the process of interviewing a subject requires that you build rapport. One tactic involved starting off with friendly banter and saving the more serious issues for later in the conversation once rapport has been established. The focus being, to get the subject to feel comfortable and trust you so they in turn would be honest and forthcoming with their answers. However, in this case, it seemed like Roxanne was trying to build rapport with me for some reason. Throughout the interview, she continually leaned forward allowing me a generous glimpse of her rather abundant décolletage. She smiled a lot. Maybe a little too much. Whenever I said something funny she laughed a little bit too hard and a little bit too long, even briefly placing her hand on my knee. I thought perhaps Roxanne was attempting to steer the investigation. Steering is a phrase used by investigators to describe a subject attempting to influence or push the investigation in a particular direction for their own purposes.

Towards the very end of the interview I asked Roxanne if Roy had any contact with foreign nationals. She threw her head back and laughed as if the question itself was preposterous. "No. Of course not, silly!" She then paused, leaned forward and looked up at me rather coyly. She flashed her long, thick, dark eyelashes and her not-so-innocent baby blue eyes and said, "Is there anything I can do to make sure he gets the job?" And right then, before I had a chance to respond to her question, she did something totally unexpected. She suddenly spread her legs revealing she wasn't wearing any underwear.

This was certainly a first. She did it so abruptly and so matter-of-factly that it startled me. I couldn't believe what I was seeing. I now realized that her lack of wearing a bra was not simply a fashion choice or because of the intense Texas heat and humidity. "Uh" I stammered. It took a few seconds for me to get the words out. "Uh, no. This isn't a job interview." I reminded her. "This is an investigation for a government security clearance. The best thing you can do to help Roy…" I paused and pointed to her, waving my finger to suggest she close her legs, "… is answer all my questions truthfully."

I don't know whether she was embarrassed or angry or both. But she suddenly got a very serious look on her face and snapped her thighs shut so abruptly I think I heard bone cartilage crack. The final few minutes of our conversation were icy cold. She was suddenly devoid of her willing smile and carefree attitude. I hurried through the rest of the interview as quickly as I could, then interviewed Roy and then got the heck out of there. I remember walking out to my car in the bright, flat Texas sunshine and saying out loud, "I cannot believe that just happened."

Later that afternoon I reported the incident to Wanda, although she didn't seem too surprised. She asked if I thought Roy had put Roxanne up to it. If so, that was a very serious allegation. However, based on all my contact with him, he had been strictly business. All my other sources, both those provided by Roy and those I developed on my own, stated that he was a stand-up guy. I told Wanda that I didn't think so. It just wasn't his style. The girl, on the other hand, was only eighteen years old. She was young and immature and probably thought she was just helping her boyfriend. Wanda told me to document everything just as it had happened and let her know if Roxanne contacted me in the future for any reason.

One thing was for sure, this job was going to be interesting.

CHAPTER 8

DYING WITH YOUR EYES OPEN

Former New York City Police Commissioner Bernard Kerik once said, "Going to prison is like dying with your eyes open." This is something I would see in the tired, drawn-out eyes of the inmates in the many prisons I visited, as well as in the eyes of some of the correctional officers who watched over them. Kerik would know. After an illustrious career with the New York City Police Department he spent four years in federal prison for tax fraud and making false statements.

I would go on to spend a great deal of time in numerous state and federal prisons during my tenure with USIS. The very first prison I visited was FMC Carswellliv, a federal prison for women with medical and mental health issues. It sits on the grounds of the Naval Air Station Fort Worth Joint Readiness Baselv on the far west side of Ft. Worth, Texas. Lynette "Squeaky" Frommelvi, the Manson Family member who attempted to assassinate President Gerald R. Ford in 1975, was incarcerated there at the time. FMC Carswell was also my first exposure to the BOP. Many of the national security background investigations I conducted involved the BOP. Most involved the periodic reinvestigation of current correctional officers and other staff members required by the government.

The very first time I went through security and entered the prison grounds was a bit surreal. After parking I entered the reception area and approached an octagon-shaped, glass-enclosed control booth. I could see two uniformed federal correctional officers in their starched white shirts and navy-blue pants sitting inside, monitoring a large security console. There were several security monitors flickering on the wall and a stack of black, hand-held, Motorola two-way radios resting in chargers. There were also numerous sets of large brass keys on the wall. I held my federal credentials against the glass window and then heard a loud buzzer as he pressed a large red button on his console. I turned to my left and watched as a heavy steel and reinforced glass electric door slowly slid open. I stepped inside and found myself in a small space about five feet square between two sets of security doors. The first door then began to slowly close until I heard a very loud metallic "thunk." In retrospect, it's funny how that sound affected me. I realized that I was now inside a federal prison and I wasn't getting out unless someone on the outside opened that door again. With the first door securely closed I waited as the second steel and glass door began to slowly slide open. For security measures, both doors were never opened at the same time. I finally stepped past the second door and onto the prison grounds. I'm not sure what I expected it to look like, but for some reason, it reminded me of the campus of a small junior college.

With my transfer to Huntsville, I spent the majority of my time visiting many of the Texas state prisons in the surrounding area. The first was The Huntsville Unit. It was built in 1849, prior to the Civil War. It was the very first penitentiary in Texas and became known as The Walls, due to the fifteen-foot red brick walls which still surround it to this day. Captured Union soldiers were housed there during the Civil War. The prison sits on about a four-acre plot and is only two blocks from the Huntsville town square. Former guests have included the Old West outlaw gunfighter John Wesley Hardin,lvii Hawaiian bounty hunter and reality television star Duane "Dog the Bounty Hunter" Chapman[lviii] and Texas drug kingpin Fred Carrasco[lix], just to name a few.

I stepped into the front entrance of The Walls and could immediately smell the disinfectant, a smell I would grow accustomed to. It seemed that all state prisons in Texas used the same brand of disinfectant. I walked through the air-conditioned administrative offices up front and passed two separate security doors. I then found myself in a very large room with a long corridor in the center and two vast holding cells on either side of the hall. The two holding cells had long benches running the length of each cell. They were used to temporarily hold inmates who were either on their way to court or were being transferred to other state prisons. Hung on the walls behind both large cells was a collection of artwork painted by inmates over the years. I was absolutely stunned by the obvious talent and the remarkable quality of the artwork. Many of the pieces belonged in a museum. I was immediately struck with the thought that such incredible talent had failed to reach its God-given potential.

The Walls houses the Texas death house where the death penalty is administered. Death row itself, however, is about an hour away at the Allan B. Polunsky Unit, near Livingston, Texas. I had been there several times and had no desire to go back. Inmates on death row reside in building twelve and wear the same white prison clothes that all Texas inmates wear. Although their prison garb has a large black "DR" in block letters on the back of their shirts.

Back at the Walls I met up with Sergeant Sam Cook. He had short blonde hair and looked a lot like the comedian Jim Gaffigan. Despite where he worked he was cheerful and had an infectious sense of humor. He wore the same grey state correctional officer uniform all the officers wore. We would fast become friends. Sam had worked for years as a training officer for the TDCJ. As a result, he knew many of the state correctional officers that had applied for positions with the BOP. It seems the federal government paid correctional officers more and provided better benefits. Because Sam knew these officers, I was able to use him as a source for my background investigations.

Not all the Texas correctional officers I had contact with were helpful or even civil. I once traveled to Lovelady, Texas to interview the warden at TDCJ's Eastham Unit. Called "The Ham," by inmates, Clyde Barrow was once incarcerated there. He was released in 1932 and traveled to Dallas where he met a woman named Bonnie Parker. Bonnie and Clyde would meet their fate two short years later on a lonely rural road in Louisiana. They were ambushed and shot to death by legendary Texas Ranger Frank Hamer and four other Texas law enforcement officers.

Upon my arrival, I showed my federal credentials at the gate and was escorted to the warden's office. I had been warned about Warden Buford Ellis before I arrived. He was well known in the TDCJ system as being a cantankerous and difficult person to deal with. But he was Warden over one of the toughest state prisons in the system and was praised for keeping everything in order. When his secretary Violet asked if I had an appointment I knew there was going to be a problem. I rarely made appointments. It was counterintuitive to the investigatory process. I needed to surprise the people I interviewed so they would be caught off guard and not have time to prepare their statement. Warden Ellis wasn't happy about it. He was a short man with a grey buzz haircut and reddish skin. He wore an old suit that looked about a size too small and he spoke in a deep baritone voice. I wanted to tell him the 1970's called, and they wanted their suit back, but I didn't think that would help my situation. As it turned out, nothing would have. He would not allow me to interview him. I explained that I was conducting a national security background investigation on a former TDCJ captain who had applied for a position with the BOP. I could've told him I was selling a subscription to Sports Illustrated. Ellis didn't care. He pretty much ignored me. He said, "I'm not giving a statement" and then walked out of his own office leaving me standing there alone.

During one of my many visits to The Walls, Sam Cook offered to show me the death house. We walked through a chain link security gate into a separate door in the northeast corner of the prison into the death house. I walked in and found three small holding cells on my left where inmates are brought about forty-eight hours before they are put to death. Across from the cells are a couple of folding chairs and a small table holding several volumes of the Bible in both English and Spanish. The door that leads to the death chamber is to the right and is painted the same institutional green, as is the interior of the cinderblock room. I could smell that same disinfectant. The whole place was clean, like a hospital. As I entered the death chamber I was struck by how small the room was; barely nine feet square. In the center of the room, about waist high level was a metal table covered with a thin mattress and pillow. It looked very much like a gurney but there were no wheels. Instead it was supported by a single, thick metal support column in the center. I found the cold institutional look of the death chamber in direct contrast with the pure, white cotton sheet and pillowcase covering the mattress and small pillow.

There were five, thick, yellowish-white leather straps interspersed equally from the head of the mattress down to the foot. They looked very much like belts. There were two additional straps on padded arm rests which extended out from both the left and right sides near the head of the gurney. Additionally, there was a small, wooden set of steps inmates use to climb up onto the gurney. It was also painted the same institutional green. There were three windows that offered a view of the death chamber from three separate rooms. The window on the left is where state officials administer lethal injection by means of the drug Pentobarbital. On the right are two separate rooms. The first is for the victim's family members; the second is for the inmate's family. Both windows have curtains that are closed once the death penalty has been carried out.

Regardless of one's feelings about the death penalty, it was sobering to see the death chamber. It was used several times during my stay in Huntsville. On June 22, 2000, a thirty-eight-year-old African-American named Gary Graham was put to death in that room at 8:49 p.m. for the 1981 murder of Bobby Lambert. At the time of the murder Graham was eighteen years old and on a ten-day crime spree. During those ten days, his charges included several armed robberies, attempted murder, several assaults and a rape. He was eventually captured when the elderly woman he raped and tortured was able to wrestle the gun away from him and call the police.

Graham's case was nothing short of a media spectacle. He had been on death row for nineteen years and had vigorously pursued every possible legal means of relief he could, including taking his case all the way to the U.S. Supreme Court. When his appeals ended, then-Texas Governor George W. Bush, the presumptive

Republican presidential candidate at the time, refused to grant a stay of execution stating that Graham had "...full and fair access to the courts, including the Supreme Court."

Later that afternoon, on the very day Graham would be put to death, I walked out of a meeting with TDCJ officials at their offices on 12th Street directly across from The Walls. What I saw next can best be described as organized chaos. The roads around the prison had been closed and were blocked with police barricades. There were several television news vans and reporters from all the major networks. Over two-hundred local law enforcement officers, including Texas state troopers and over two dozen Texas Rangers formed a perimeter around The Walls. It was pure bedlam. Bianca Jagger, the Nation of Islam and the New Black Panther Party demonstrated on the northeast side of the prison. Some of the protestors were burning the U.S. Flag. I saw the Reverend Jesse Jackson in a grey suit walking among the protesters. Several of the Black Panthers were strolling down the street wearing camouflage pants, black berets and carrying shotguns. The crowd on the northwest side of the prison was comprised of the media and various other protesters including the Ku Klux Klan. Klan members protested in their white Klan robes waving the Confederate battle flag. It was like something out of a Hollywood movie. In the end, it was all for naught. Graham was put to death, facing the judgement of God and his victims in that small room in the corner of The Walls.

The next day everything was back to normal. It was just another hot and humid June morning. Prison trustees in their white state prison clothes roamed outside The Walls picking up trash and trimming hedges. In the faint distance, I could hear a lawn mower. It was as if the chaotic events of the previous day had never really happened, as if it were all a dream. Thirty-nine more people would be put to death before the year was over.

I returned to The Walls several days later early in the morning to conduct more interviews. After parking my car in a nearby parking lot, I walked down 12th Street toward the entrance and noticed a large gathering of people on the grassy lawn of the TDCJ office building directly across the street from The Walls. The group consisted of mostly adult women and children. I was puzzled by what I first thought to be an impromptu gathering. They stood there as if they were waiting for something. Right about that time an exterior door that I never knew existed opened on the northeast corner of The Walls. Suddenly, about seventy-five men, all walking in a single file line, exited and began walking west down 12th Street in my direction. The men wore outdated and poorly-fitting street clothes donated by local churches. Several of them broke from the line and ran towards the women and children waiting on the nearby lawn. I suddenly realized the men were inmates being released from prison and the women and children on the lawn were family members. I could see several of the women on their tiptoes, moving their heads left and right as they peered through the crowd looking for their loved one. I heard shouts of "I see him!" and "There's daddy!" There were plenty of hugs and tears as wives were reunited with husbands and children reunited with their fathers. It was quite a sight to behold. They say that when a man goes to prison, his family, at least metaphorically, goes with him.

Seeing that long line of men at The Walls reminded me of another long line. But it was in another time and another place. It was almost 10 years earlier in late

February 1991. I was part of a heavily armed military convoy traveling northeast on highway 50 in northern Saudi Arabia. The ground combat operations in the Persian Gulf War had begun. My unit had just left the Saudi Arabian town of Hafar Al Batin. We were on our way to Ar Ruqi, a small town on the border of Saudi Arabia. From there we would cross over into Iraq and eventually move on to Kuwait to intercept the Iraqi Republican Guard. Our convoy stretched out for miles on this narrow two-lane paved road. There was nothing but miles and miles of vast desert on either side of the highway as far as the eye could see. I remember the smell of fear in the air. The clouds were low and dark; almost menacing, as if they were somehow privy to what lay ahead for us. Up until this time the war had seemed like a distant event I listened to on the radio, as if it was happening to someone else. Then I saw what was coming down the road. Coming from the opposite direction and moving south was another convoy. It consisted of hundreds of cars and trucks of all makes and models. Each vehicle was packed with clothes, mattresses and appliances. This convoy was full of Saudi's and Kuwaiti's fleeing the war zone with all of their belongings. It was the first time the war had become real to me. I was a solider and I was just doing my job. But I now saw how the war had a tremendous effect on many people outside of my small mortar crew. When I saw those men walk out of The Walls that morning and embrace their families, I had similar thoughts.

The seventy-five men released that day were part of the over 20,000 inmates released from prison every year in Texas. The ex-convicts who didn't have family waiting for them walked two blocks to the small Huntsville Greyhound Bus station at the corner of 12th Street and Avenue J. There, they presented a prison transportation voucher to the ticket counter. They then boarded a Greyhound bus for their Texas county of residence and a second chance at a new life if they could manage to make it so.

Of course, not everyone got out of prison. I was once at the old Missouri State Penitentiarylx off Lafayette Street in Jefferson City interviewing an inmate. He had been convicted of sexual assault and was serving an eight-year sentence. His public defender told me that based on the trial evidence, "he's probably guilty but go check it out anyway."

I arrived there early the next morning and, after going through security, entered a small interview room. Shortly thereafter Lamar Caruthers walked in wearing handcuffs. He was a tall, lanky black male. He was serving time for rape. He was represented by a public defender and I told Lamar I was his investigator. It goes against prison etiquette to ask an inmate why he's in prison. If they want you to know they'll tell you. Plenty of them will tell you they didn't do it, whatever it is. I already knew what Lamar's crime was. But he said he was innocent.

"I didn't rape that girl." By girl, he meant woman. The victim was his on-again, off-again girlfriend; a white female in her early thirties named Stormy. "She was all into it, you see," he explained further. Like many inmates, Caruthers had dropped out of school in the sixth grade. His use of English was poor and stilted. I had to gather specific details if we were going to find exculpatory evidencelxi. "We was all getting into it," he said. "And right before I was about to finish, know what I'm saying…she said stop. But I couldn't. So, I just finished." It sounded somewhat dubious to me, but Lamar had been convicted and was sitting in prison.

viewed Stormy later. She was a heavy-set woman with dirty blonde ed nose and tattoo of the Tasmanian Devil on her left bicep. She essentially told the same story but volunteered that she began saying "stop" a little earlier in the act. I looked at the report from the medical exam filed after the rape and found that it didn't reflect the bruising, tearing and other signs consistent with sexual assault. Stormy did admit that Lamar could've thought her saying "no" was all part of the sex play. But he was the one sitting in prison while she sat in front of me smoking one cigarette after another.

I'm not saying I believed Lamar. I'm not saying I didn't believe Stormy. I think race was probably a factor in the conviction. What I am saying is that there is often a fine line between the truth and how people view the truth. When taking statements, you must avoid falling into the trap of believing everything you hear. It was Benjamin Franklin who said, "Believe none of what you hear, and only half of what you see." A private investigator will hear different points of view from everyone they interview. The truth is always somewhere in between. I'm not talking about the principle of moderation; I'm suggesting that everyone comes to the table with their own prejudices and experiences. To understand the truth of why and how something occurred, you must first seek to understand the people involved. In the end, Lamar stayed in prison.

One of the nicest prisons I ever visited was the minimum security federal prison camp for women in Bryan, Texas. FPC Bryan, as the BOP labeled it, is located on Ursuline Avenue in a quiet, beautiful neighborhood of winding residential streets and lovely homes shaded by large Live Oak trees. The prison is on 37 acres and is a collection of white stucco buildings with red terra cotta roofs.

This is not Alcatraz. In fact, it looks more like a private school than a federal prison. There are no looming guard towers or roaming security patrols. There isn't even a fence. This minimum-security prison holds about 900 female inmates at any given time. Former guests have included Lea Fastow, wife of Andrew Fastow, the former CFO of Enron, as well as several disgraced female politicians little known outside their local areas. Troy Gilchrist, the associate warden, once told me, "All of the women in here are here because of a man." Indeed. Most of the women were incarcerated for money laundering, credit card fraud or drug charges, mostly due to their involvement with their drug dealer boyfriends or husbands.

Aside from periodic reinvestigations of the federal correctional officers, I also handled investigations of the medical personnel, which included the five gynecologists on staff. I arrived in College Station one morning to conduct a Personal Subject Interview, or PRSI[lxii], on Gwen Robinson, a nurse with the U.S. Public Health Service[lxiii] who worked at the prison. The PRSI is a comprehensive personal interview an applicant must submit to in order to obtain a government security clearance. In reviewing her SF 86[lxiv] form prior to the interview, I discovered she had been stationed at four different federal prisons within the preceding twelve years. During those twelve years, she had moved her residence four times. I also saw that Gwen's current roommate, a woman named Chynna Swenson, had been her roommate at all four of the previous residences. I discussed this with my supervisor, Wanda Ashworth. Her feeling was that Gwen and Chynna were possibly lesbians. This was, in and of itself, immaterial. However, at this time the U.S. government had specific rules I was required to follow with regards to homosexuals and security clearances. There was nothing precluding them from holding a clearance. That was not the issue. The government's principal concern was who knew about the individual's lifestyle and whether or not they were vulnerable to blackmail because of it. For example, if it was common knowledge the individual was gay and family and friends were aware, then the government assumed they would be less susceptible to extortion or acting under duress. If no one was aware of their lifestyle, then the question remained, was it something that could be used to coerce them into revealing classified information or acting under duress in the prison environment. Fortunately, I didn't have to make those decisions. And personally, I really didn't care. My feelings then and now were whether or not someone was gay or not gay was a personal issue and none of my business, nor the governments for that matter. But the government had specific regulations when it came to security clearances and I was required to follow them. The only caveat was that due to privacy and legal issues, I could not openly ask Gwen whether she was a lesbian. I had to get Gwen to admit to the lifestyle. Once she brought it up, then I could ask who knew and whether it was something that might make her susceptible to blackmail or acting under duress.

I met Gwen and Chynna late one afternoon at their home in a nice, older neighborhood right across from Kyle Field, home of the Texas A&M Aggies Football team. Interestingly, they looked very much alike. They were both twenty-nine-year-old white females and both were employed as nurses; Gwen at the prison and Chynna at St. Joseph's Hospital in Bryan. Furthermore, they were about the same height and weight and sported identical short blond haircuts. They could've been sisters. There were pictures of them throughout their home, both professional studio portraits and photographs of them on vacation engaged in various outdoor activities together. It was clear to me they were lesbians. It was also clear that they deemed their living arrangement to be none of the government's business. No matter how I phrased the questions, they stated that they were nothing more than just roommates. Although these rules were the government's rules, I was still embarrassed to have to discuss this matter with them. Gwen had held a security clearance for several years and had a spotless record. In the end, neither would admit to being gay. I finished my interview and moved on. I wasn't going to judge them. I have a hard-enough time being me.

CHAPTER 9

YOUR SECURITY CLEARANCE IS DENIED

As I started my second year working for USIS in Huntsville, I began to handle an increasingly heavy work-load under very strict deadlines. Much of it was routine but occasionally even the routine was punctuated by the bizarre. I have a personal theory that regardless of someone's occupation, there exists a point where everything can become routine. I think it's true for police officers, Navy Seals and even for Secret Service agents on a protective detail. I discovered it to be true while conducting sensitive national security background investigations. You interview so many people there's a tendency to sometimes take what everyone says as the absolute truth. You take the statement and move on to the next one. It becomes easy to forget that people lie or, at least, stretch the truth. Historian Doris Kerns Goodwin said, "The past is not simply the past, but a prism through which the subject filters his own changing self-image." I learned that despite what people told me, not everyone was eligible for a security clearance. And that included people like Frank Hamilton.

Frank was a student at Blinn College in Bryan, Texas. He was six feet tall and possessed boyish good looks and plenty of charm to go around. Everybody loved Frank. He would soon graduate with an associate degree in criminal justice and had applied to be a police officer with the Secret Service's Uniformed Division[lxv] in Washington, D.C. I remember Frank's interview going quite well. Afterwards I followed up with both provided and developed sources to gather more information. That's when I discovered Frank was a fervent racist.

During Frank's background investigation, I developed a source named Lola who had dated him for the better part of year. We met at Burger Boy, a local hamburger joint in Bryan, not far from Blinn College. Lola was medium height and slim with long, straight blond hair which cascaded down to her shoulders. She was wearing faded Levi's blue jeans and a black short-sleeve Burger Boy polo shirt. She had just finished her shift when I arrived. We walked across the blue and white checkered linoleum floor and slid into a corner booth out of earshot from everyone. I showed her my credentials and then pulled out my green USIS flip notepad. I began to go through the same standard questions I had asked a thousand times before. I could tell Lola was tired having just completed an eight-hour shift. It was the end of my work day as well, but I still had a forty-five-minute drive back to Huntsville. Towards the end of the interview I asked her if there was anything about Frank's personal conduct that would make him unsuitable to hold a security clearance. She thought for a moment and then, in what must have been a sudden moment of clarity for her, blurted out, "Well… he's racist." That suddenly woke me up from my routine-induced brain fog.

"Excuse me?" I needed her to clarify what she meant by Frank being a racist.

She hesitated. "I don't want to get him into any trouble. But he used the word nigger all the time when we were dating" she finally said. "I think he really hates black people. He and his friends were always making fun of them and telling black jokes. They always talked about wanting to join the KKK and kill blacks."

Interesting. Especially since I had interviewed several of those so-called friends; all of whom had failed to mention this particular peccadillo. And Frank wanted to be a police officer in Washington, D.C. no less, a city where over fifty percent of the residents are African-American.

"And what about you, Lola? Is this something you approve of," I asked?

"Of course not," she said. She started to get a little perturbed. "It's actually one of the reasons we broke up. I don't think that way and I got sick and tired of hearing him go on and on about it. At first, I thought it was just a joke. But eventually I realized he was serious."

This was a grave accusation, albeit from an ex-girlfriend. But sadly, it turned out to be true. Lola provided me with the names of several other sources who corroborated her story. As a result, Frank Hamilton did not receive a security clearance and, therefore, could not accept a position with the Uniformed Division in Washington, D.C. Frank would not be the only government applicant my investigations would expose. There was also Paul.

Paul Benavidez was the youngest son of a wealthy rancher in Alpine, Texas. He had applied for a position with the U.S. Border Patrol. I headed out to this west Texas town to spend a couple of days working on his background investigation.

Alpine is a small town of about six thousand people north of Big Bend National Park and the county seat of Brewster County. The 1956 Warner Brothers movie *Giant*, was filmed nearby. It's also home to Sul Ross University where Paul received a degree in sociology. The Holland Hotel, a Texas Historic Landmark built in 1912, is on West Holland Avenue in downtown Alpine. The Century Grill, located in the hotel, serves up the best steak you'll ever have in your life. But don't make the mistake of asking for steak sauce. The chef will take offence. Besides, you won't need it. It's so good it'll make you slap your grandma.

Paul had an older brother named Earnest whom, I discovered, was anything but earnest. While conducting Paul's background investigation I tracked down Earnest's ex-wife, Sylvia. She lived in an old dilapidated mobile home surrounded by several vehicles in varying states of decay near Marfa, Texas, a small town thirty minutes west of Alpine. It was Sylvia who told me that Earnest and Paul were Coyotajes.lxvi She said they had a part-time business on the side ferrying illegal immigrants across the Texas-Mexican border for a fee. Paul's master plan was to be hired by the border patrol, thus making their smuggling job easier and infinitely more lucrative.

Initially I didn't find her story credible. Similar to Lola's accusations against Frank Hamilton, I would need some additional confirmation. Normally the government wouldn't even interview an ex-spouse, primarily because they rarely have anything good to say. However, as I continued my interviews with other sources a bigger picture began to emerge. It became abundantly clear the Benavidez brothers were indeed running a smuggling enterprise on the side. In the end, Paul was unsuccessful in receiving a security clearance or an offer from the U.S. Border Patrol.

During my time in Huntsville I was a frequent visitor to the INSlxvii office on the south side of town. It was a small non-descript single-story building off state highway 75 adjacent to the TDCJ's Goree Prison Unit. The office staffed several deportation officers. They were responsible for expatriating non-U.S.

citizens from the TDCJ system and the surrounding areas. I often spent time there conducting interviews and periodic reinvestigations of the INS employees.

During a few of my visits, Robert Macklemore, one of the many deportation officers, began to casually question me about the security clearance process. He was short, with an athletic build and had been with the INS for over ten years. I didn't give his questions much thought. I knew his periodic reinvestigation was coming up and I figured he just wanted to know what to expect. After all, it had been about five years since his last reinvestigation. Perhaps the process had changed somewhat. Still, I found the questions a little odd considering he was already well into his career and presumably had been through the process twice before. However, later I discovered that OPM had a tremendous backlog of cases. As a result, not all government employees were reinvestigated every five years as required. I ultimately shrugged it off and forgot all about it. When the time came I conducted his PRSI and everything went fine. He was honest and forthcoming, and I don't recall any issues.

Fast forward several months later. I was back at the same INS office conducting more interviews when it suddenly dawned on me I had not seen Robert around the office in the past several months. He was very friendly and always made a point of saying hello. Perhaps he had transferred. I asked one of the deportation officers about it, but my question was met with a blank stare. "No," he sheepishly replied. Something in the way he said no made me realize there was more to the story. I walked over to the office of Cindy Hayes, the supervisory agent and my point of contact in the office. And after some gentle prodding she told me the whole bizarre story.

Robert was originally from the small town of Falfurrias, Texas, and had gone back on vacation for a couple of weeks. During that time, the Border Patrol station south of Falfurrias pulled over a red 1999 Ford Escort traveling north on highway 281. The three occupants of the car turned out to be Mexicans attempting to enter the U.S. illegally. That, in and of itself, is not odd. It happens all the time. What was interesting is that when the Border Patrol ran the license plates on the Ford Escort, they discovered it was registered to a Robert Macklemore. A few more checks and they discovered Robert Macklemore was a U.S. government employee. The very same Robert Macklemore who happened to be an INS deportation officer. And yes, the very same Robert Macklemore who had recently sailed through his periodic reinvestigation. As it turned out, Robert had a business on the side. By day he was the straight-laced INS deportation officer responsible for upholding the immigration laws of the United States. By night, and apparently while on vacation, he used his experience and position to facilitate illegal immigration for a fee. He just didn't realize how much it would cost him in the end.

Of course, Robert wasn't the only government employee on the take; something I learned when I set out to conduct a periodic reinvestigation on Bobby "Skip" Becker, a Special Agent Pilot for the Drug Enforcement Administration (DEA). Skip provided surveillance and air support for the DEA intelligence and drug enforcement operations in the Houston, Texas area. He had failed to return my numerous telephone calls, which was really odd for a government employee. I ended up driving to In the Woods Aviation Service, the DEA's secret aviation hanger in Montgomery County, north of Houston. It was a non-descript building at a small airfield surrounded by the thick piney woods of East Texas. I ended up speaking with Becker's supervisor who hemmed and hawed and was initially non-committal. Once he realized I wasn't going away he finally admitted that Skip was missing. And so were hundreds of thousands of dollars in recently seized drug money. There would be no interview. I don't know if the DEA ever caught up with Skip, but I do know the Bureau of Land Management (BLM) eventually caught up with a woman named Eleanor. I know because I'm the one who caught her.

Eleanor Swift had hazel eyes and shoulder length brunette hair. She weighed closed to two hundred pounds and was no more than five feet tall. She worked for the BLM in Oklahoma, the federal agency that manages public lands. Eleanor had injured her back at work and filed a workers' compensation claim. It's what we call in the business a "slip and fall." She slipped. She fell. At work. According to her doctor she couldn't stand or walk for extended periods of time. She couldn't lift anything over 10 pounds. She remained at home and was advised to stay off her feet. But as the days turned into weeks and the weeks slowly turned into months, it became apparent that Eleanor was malingering.lxviii

Like many of the approximately 30 percent of people committing workers' compensation fraud, Eleanor began secretly working another job; thus, doubling her income. She would end up paying a rather heavy price for defrauding the US government.

Eleanor lived in a small town in rural eastern Oklahoma and the word eventually got around that she was fine. There was nothing physically wrong with her, except she was receiving a bi-weekly workers' compensation checks AND a pay check. It was while she was sitting at home on workers' compensation that Eleanor decided to follow through on her dream of owning her own restaurant. So that's exactly what she did. I was working for USIS in Dallas at the time and was asked to go check her out. I got behind the wheel of my trusty surveillance vehicle and drove north to Oklahoma on state highway 69 to uncover the truth about Eleanor.

When it comes to surveillance, things rarely go as planned. The whole process can take days and can be unpredictable. That is the nature of surveillance. Eleanor proved to be the exception. As I drove into the small town of Atoka, Oklahoma, I drove right past her restaurant, "Eleanor's Home Cooking." As if by chance, I happened to glance to my left when I saw her walking out the back door of the establishment carrying a heavy wooden crate of tomatoes. So much for her inability to carry over 10 pounds and walk or stand for any length of time. By the time I did a U-turn and retraced my steps, she had already gone back inside. I quickly set up a surveillance on her restaurant. Thirty minutes later she exited the building and climbed into a silver Ford F350 pickup truck. At barely five feet, she struggled to climb up into the cab. I got it on video and then followed her to a self-serve car wash. Once there, I observed her scrub, brush, wash and vacuum the vehicle for thirty minutes. All of this physical activity was well beyond the scope of her alleged injury. She eventually drove home for the evening and I decided to check into my hotel and get a fresh start in the morning.

Early the next morning, I had a nice breakfast at Bledsoe's Diner and then slipped over to the Atoka County Courthouse. At the courthouse, I retrieved copies of Eleanor's business license and DBA, further documenting proof of her little enterprise. My next stop was the Atoka County Times, the local newspaper. I made copies of news stories describing the grand opening of Eleanor's Home Cooking. One of the stories was a rather touching personal interest piece about her struggles to make her dream of restaurant entrepreneurship come true. There on the front page was a photograph of Eleanor smiling and holding a giant pair of scissors for the ribbon cutting and grand opening with the Atoka County Chamber of Commerce.

After all that work, it was time for lunch. I suddenly had a craving for some home cooking and I knew just the place. I got back to my car and turned the wheel towards Eleanor's restaurant. As I walked in, the wooden floor boards creaked and gave. I sat down behind a wooden table with a blue tablecloth which afforded me a clear view of the kitchen. The place was very nice. It had an old rustic, log cabin feel to it, similar to Cracker Barrel. It was a comfortable restaurant for the comfort food that she served.

After a couple of minutes Eleanor approached my table with a notepad and pencil in hand to take my order. We exchanged pleasantries, although she had no idea who I was or why I was there. As she took my order I peppered her with a series of questions. Her answers were later documented in my report. On the surface, it seemed as if I was just asking casual questions. In reality, she was providing a statement. She just didn't know it. I verified that she owned the restaurant and had been in business for about three months. I confirmed that she worked ten to twelve hours a day, six days a week with barely a break. She admitted that most of that time was spent on her feet. She also stated that she was not only the owner, but also the main cook and one of the waitresses. I had to admit, aside from her defrauding of government funds, she had a great work ethic.

Upon my return to Dallas, I filed my video and report. I didn't hear any initial feedback about the investigation. However, about two months later I received a letter of commendation from the head of the BLM region where Eleanor had worked. I found out she was charged with fraud and eventually sent to federal prison. German philosopher Friedrich Nietzsche once said, "The lie is a condition of life." Obviously, something Eleanor Swift would eventually come to understand and pay dearly for.

As bad as Eleanor's fraud was, her activities paled in comparison to Vincent Lewiston's. He would lose his security clearance for something that had happened ten years before. Vincent was tall and thin with jet black hair and ice blue eyes that seemed to look right through you. He worked for a U.S. government defense contractor at the Idaho National Laboratory west of Idaho Falls in the south-east corner of Idaho. Vincent held a Q clearance with the DOE and had been at the labs for almost two decades. During one of his regular re-investigations his ex-wife Rita happen to be interviewed. Rita said Vincent had sexually abused their two daughters ten years earlier.

As I previously mentioned, statements from ex-spouses were usually taken with a grain of salt, if they're taken at all. In fact, the government often declines to interview the ex-wife or ex-husband. They're rarely capable of providing a balanced and objective picture of the subject. Vincent and Rita's divorce had been particularly acrimonious, and she was known to be a tippler. Her adult beverage of choice: peach schnapps. Yet another reason why Rita's statements seemed unreliable and didn't garner the attention that in retrospect they should have.

As it turned out, Vincent and Rita's case was eerily similar to that of John A. Walker, Jr. Walker was a U.S. Navy Chief Warrant Officer who turned over highly classified material to the KGB from 1968 until his retirement from the Navy in 1983. Walker had stolen classified information and operated with impunity for fifteen years. His ex-wife, Barbara Crowley, was aware of his espionage activities but she was an alcoholic and was initially not interviewed for the reasons I have just described. When the FBI finally did interview her, they initially brushed her off as a bitter drunk. The Special Agent sent to interview her stated she was angry at her ex-husband and willing to say anything to ruin his career.

For much the same reason, Rita was never interviewed during Vincent's prior periodic reinvestigations. However, this time she was listed as a source to be interviewed. The government finally decided to consider her allegations to see if her story could be corroborated. The logical place to start would be with the two daughters. I was assigned to interview Tiffany, the youngest daughter.

Tiffany Lewiston was now nineteen years old and attending the University of Texas at Arlington. I met her on campus and we retreated to a sound proof study room on the third floor of the Central Library. She was very petite and had brunette hair that she pulled back and wore in a ponytail. I sensed an overall feeling of sadness about her. She wore a bright pink hoodie and faded Levi's blue jeans and carried a navy-blue backpack. Tiffany looked like a typical college student.

The first rule of interviewing is to be prepared. I knew the case backwards and forwards. However, just like the background investigation with Gwen Robinson at FPC Bryan, I had to abide within certain privacy and legal constraints. Vincent had rights. So far, the abuse was considered just an allegation. I couldn't simply ask Tiffany, "Did your father sexually abuse you?" Maybe it wasn't true. Vincent had a long illustrious career and a spotless record. If the sexual abuse did occur, I had to get Tiffany to voluntarily admit it, and that's not easy. For that to happen I first needed to build rapport.

As I interviewed her we talked about her schooling. We talked about Texas. We talked about her part-time job as a dental hygienist for a nearby dental office. It was painstakingly difficult, but I slowly found common ground with her. I also began mirroring her body language.

Much of communication is non-verbal. Mirroring is a non-verbal way of building rapport with your subject. You mirror the subject's body movements, as well as the speed and timbre of their speech patterns. You begin to sound and move like them. You become like them. It involves copying their gestures, hand motions, facial expressions, how they sit and even how they speak. It's not done in such a way as to be patently obvious. It's subtler than that. Tiffany was from a small town in a rural area. Because of that she tended to speak slower and more deliberately than people in the city, who tend to speak faster and more direct. I also left the difficult questions until later in the interview once I had built rapport.

Interviews involving sexual abuse are like any other type of interview in that they require specifics. It is not enough for the subject to say "he touched me" or "he molested me." Those words are not specific. They have different meanings to different people. Unfortunately, an investigator must gather specifics to ascertain the exact nature and degree of the abuse so that there is no difficulty understanding what happened. The obvious questions are where, when, how often, and so forth. And I had to convince Tiffany, a stranger I had just met twenty minutes prior, to reveal these painful, sordid memories. Memories she had no doubt spent the last several years trying to forget.

As it turns out, Vincent's ex-wife Rita had been right all along. She may have been a drunk. But sadly, what she had been saying about Vincent was true. The government had been dropping the ball. I began to talk to Tiffany about her relationship with her father and, while not divulging any specific details, stated, "I want you to know I've spoken with your mother." I inserted a psychological pause allowing my words to silently hang in the air like a subtle red flag waiting to be recognized. I intimated that her mother had told me everything; thus, leading Tiffany to believe that I knew about the sexual abuse. In the end, I got her to open up and provide details. It first began with her older sister Sherry. Tiffany became aware of it because their father would come into the bedroom late at night, take Sherry by the hand and walk out of the bedroom.

Later, when Sherry turned 16 years old and began to resist, Vincent turned his depraved attention to Tiffany and began to sexually abuse her. It began when she was 13 years old and continued for about two years. Tiffany could not recall the exact dates. She admitted that it happened about once a week throughout that time frame. He did not have intercourse with her, but instead fondled her breasts and her genitals. He forced her to perform oral sex on him and then would do the same on her. I asked Tiffany when and how it stopped. Again, she couldn't remember exactly. Much of her memory from that time was understandably hazy; like a thick fog. But who could blame her? No one would want to remember such a terrible ordeal.

She seemed to think that her mother had returned from a bar late one night, drunk as usual, and walked in on them. In her state of inebriation Rita threatened Vincent and said if he ever touched their daughters again she'd shoot him first and call the police second. She also made a few other comments about removing a certain body part with a pair of rusty scissors. He got the message. The next morning her father went to work, and Tiffany and Sherry went to school. The incident was never mentioned again, not even by her mother. It was as if nothing had ever happened. Sometimes Tiffany thought that her mother coming home and walking in on her and her father was all a dream. However, within the next six months her father moved out and he and Rita eventually divorced. That was the last time Tiffany and Sherry had any contact with their father.

Tiffany held her head low and stared down at the floor. Enormous tears silently streamed down her cheeks as she cried softly and related to me the horrible events of the past. Each word was clear and enunciated. Her brave words seemed to hang in the eerie silence of the sound-proof study room. Everything she said about that awful nightmare hung over her head like an impenetrable cloud. She zipped up her hoodie and put the hood over her head attempting to hide from me, the world and the awful experiences of so many years ago. I wanted to comfort her and tell her that everything would be okay. But that would not have been appropriate. Still, it was difficult to sit there and watch her suffer; to know that I was responsible for opening up these old wounds and that no one was there to provide her any comfort.

After the interview, I walked across campus towards my car with mixed feelings. I was both relieved and glad I had been able to get the truth from Tiffany. I had done my job. But, at the same time I hated myself for having to remind her of the sexual abuse and make her relive the pain of those years all over again. It was pain that she had no doubt spent her short life struggling to forget. But I was required to investigate her father. Upon hearing her story, I believed her. I absolutely knew he would lose his security clearance and no longer be employed by the DOE. There was also no statute of limitations on sexual assault of a child under 16 years of age in Idaho. It had taken ten years, but Vincent's past had finally caught up with him. He just didn't know it yet. My interview with Tiffany Lewiston was successful. But it came at a rather high price.

CHAPTER 10

CITIZEN FOUR AND THE DEMISE OF USIS

Patriot Day. Every American knows where they were and what they were doing on Tuesday, September 11, 2001. For me and so many others it began just like another day. But the events of that day would go on to be indelibly marked upon our consciousness forever. It was a beautiful and brisk fall morning. I was at the U.S. Post Office in Huntsville, Texas when a customer suddenly burst in and said an airplane had hit the World Trade Center in New York City. My initial thought was that a small private plane had crashed into one of the towers. I thought perhaps the pilot had become ill or disoriented, although that seemed a bit implausible. I rushed out to my car in the parking lot and turned on the radio. It was 9:03 a.m. I sat there with the driver's side door still open, as I heard the live reports of United Airlines flight 175 smashing into the south tower of the World Trade Center. That's when I knew it wasn't an accident. If the odds of one plane hitting the World Trade Center were rare, then two planes hitting had to signal something malevolent. America was under attack.

I had already scheduled an interview with a school teacher at New Waverly High School off state highway 75 in New Waverly, Texas. After hearing the initial news reports on my car radio, I hesitated, unsure of how to proceed. At this point I really didn't understand the magnitude of the attack so I continued with my work day. When I arrived thirty minutes later I found the school in lockdown mode. It was during my short drive from Huntsville to New Waverly that a third airplane,

American Airlines flight 77 crashed into the Pentagon killing all fifty-nine people aboard. One hundred and twenty-five military and civilian personnel were also killed in the Pentagon.

I had to show my government credentials to the principal before he would unlock the door and let me in. The students and staff were sheltering in place. The attack was unprecedented. Nothing of this magnitude had happened in my lifetime. Not since Pearl Harbor had the U.S. homeland been so viciously attacked. We were all stunned, and no one knew what to do. The principal was carrying a two-way radio in his right hand and as we walked to his office he turned to me and said, "You picked a bad day for your interview."

This was before social media, smart phones and the ubiquitous nature of the internet. Radio and television still provided the majority of our information. As a result, I continued to be glued to my car radio as I went through the motions of work that day, but my efforts felt hollow. It was difficult to interview people and gather public records and carry on normal conversations as if nothing was happening. My activities paled in comparison to what was going on in those other parts of the country. Earlier that day, Wanda, my manager in Dallas, advised us to continue with work as usual. But in her defense, this was before all the terrorist attacks had been carried out and the enormity of the events could be comprehended. By late afternoon I recognized the futility of my efforts and turned my car toward home. It wasn't until I got home that evening that I finally saw the news reports on television. I remember standing in my apartment looking at the television. I was horrified.

Because of 9/11, my work slowed down for the next several weeks as all of America tried to grapple with what had happened. Airlines, banks, shopping centers and schools all closed, at least temporarily. The tragedy had occurred on a Tuesday and we didn't know if there would be a second wave of attacks. Later that week I received a memorandum from USIS. I was directed to go about my work as best I could but to be sensitive to what everyone was going through. Yet, even weeks later it was difficult to just sit there and interview people. Everyone was so deeply affected by those events.

The 11th of September eventually gave way to a rather somber Christmas season. The fires from the World Trade Center continued to burn into December and served as a constant reminder we had been attacked. The smoke could be seen for miles, even from space. By the beginning of 2002 things slowly began to go back to normal. It wouldn't be for another 10 years until Osama Bin Laden, head of the Islamic terrorist group Al-Qaeda and the person ultimately responsible for the attack on 9/11, was killed. He was cornered on the third floor of his Abbottabad, Pakistan residence in early May of 2011. Bin Laden met his fate when Senior Chief Petty Officer Robert "Rob" J. O'Neill of Seal Team 6 put three bullets into his head. He then keyed his radio and uttered the phrase, "For God and country…Geronimo, Geronimo, Geronimo."

Early in the year I ended up traveling on an investigative detail to Ft. Worth where I took several statements from employees at the Lockheed Martin plant. After interviewing one subject, he asked me if I wanted a tour. At the time, the F-16 fighter jet was manufactured at the facility. Production took place in an immense warehouse. At the beginning of the production line the F-16 was no more than a piece of metal small enough to hold in your hand. As we progressed down the assembly line it slowly began to be recognizable and take the shape of a fighter jet. Knowing this jet was sold to U.S. allies I asked if he ever ran into problems. He chuckled and said, "Well, we have to keep the Saudi's and the Israeli's from running into each other whenever they visit."

I also spent time at NASA's Johnson Space Center (JSC) in the Clear Lake area south of Houston. I ended up conducting several national security background investigations on the NASA engineers who worked on the robotic arm of the space shuttle. The robotic arm itself was manufactured by a Canadian firm but NASA had their own engineers working on it at JSC. I guess I expected the offices at NASA to look futuristic, like something out of Star Wars. But, considering that they were built in the 1960's, they looked like any other government office. It was a collection of desks, cubicles, computers and dry erase whiteboards. Getting past NASA's front door, on the other hand, was another matter, especially since many of my interviews were supposed to be unannounced. The protocol was to surprise the individual and not allow them time to prepare an organized statement or discuss the visit with the subject of the investigation. Fortunately, once again my federal badge and credentials greased the skids and I was ushered in. And like my back-stage tour of the Lockheed-Martin plant, I received a similar tour of JSC.

Probably the most interesting and secure location I ever visited was the U.S. Bureau of Engraving and Printing'slxix western currency facility located in Ft. Worth. It was off Blue Mound Road but finding the public entrance itself was a challenge. It was almost as if they were attempting to dissuade anyone from visiting. The only way to enter the facility is if someone was expecting you. That made my surprise visits infinitely more difficult. It took about thirty minutes at their security office before they could even get the person on the line and explain why I was there to see him. From there I drove to another security gate where armed federal security officers used a mirror to look underneath my car. They had a dog sniff around my vehicle for explosives and even asked me to pop the trunk and hood, so they could search there as well. And keep in mind I was carrying U.S government credentials. After that I still had to go through a third security entrance once I reached the actual facility. I was forced to empty my pockets, hand over my cell phone for the duration of my visit and walk through a magnetometer. I then sat on a plush couch in the lobby and waited for the employee to meet me. The whole process, including the subsequent interview, took all morning.

After the interview, the employee took me up to a glass-enclosed, suspended walkway that allowed visitors to look down on the production floor of the facility. This was the extent of my back-stage tour. I've never seen so much money in my life. Stacks of money and wooden pallets full of $100-dollar bills littered the entire floor. "Money makes people crazy," my guide told me. "Someone's always trying to figure out a way to get some of it out of here." His comments were still on my mind as I walked out the building and back to the parking lot in the early afternoon. It must have been time for a shift change. Employees were pouring in from the parking lot carrying large plastic see-through tote bags with their lunch and wallet contained therein. Just one more security measure to make sure money wasn't stolen.

But there's always a way. Even with their strict security, in 2006 a government employee named David Faison would eventually steal $67,000.00 worth of uncut, unfinished one-hundred-dollar bills. He dropped the bills in slot machines at casinos throughout New Jersey, Delaware and West Virginia, exchanging them for legitimate bills. He was eventually caught on surveillance after casino management discovered the unfinished bills lacked serial numbers or the U.S. Treasury seal.

I would go on to develop a multitude of issues involving the subjects of my investigations. Many of them had problems such as drug or alcohol abuse, civil lawsuits and various other types of arrests; like the mystery of the vanishing lawyer, Melissa Sloan. Though it turned out to not to be much of a mystery at all.

My appointment was set for Monday morning at her office in downtown Houston. Melissa was a government attorney with the U.S. Department of Labor (DOL) and it was time for her periodic reinvestigation. Up until now everything had gone as planned. I left a voice mail message late Sunday night to remind her of our appointment. I never heard back from her. That Monday I parked my car and rode a quiet elevator to the 11th floor of her office building on S. Gessner Drive. After waiting for what seemed like an inordinate amount of time, her secretary slowly sauntered over with a dejected look on her face. "I'm sorry" she said, "but we can't find her. She hasn't shown up for work this morning and she's not answering any of her phone numbers."

I went back to my office. I tried calling and emailing her throughout the day. I continued to get no response. It was as if she had simply vanished. I was under pressure to deliver timely results for the client. I was required to make some efforts towards due diligence. So, I made a couple of more phone calls and found her in five minutes flat. I couldn't believe where she was.

After finding Melissa Sloan I made a mental note to remember this little trick in the future. No, she wasn't kidnapped by a violent drug cartel and she didn't forget about the interview. She wasn't at home. She wasn't at work or in court. And she wasn't dead. Melissa Sloan, government attorney for the DOL, was in jail. She had been arrested for driving under the influence by Houston's finest on Sunday night. She was currently a guest of the city in the downtown jail. She hadn't made a phone call because she was embarrassed and didn't want anyone to know where she was. That, and the fact a DUI arrest would certainly not be good for her security clearance.

The government refers to these adverse matters, like the attorney's DUI, as *issues*. USIS reviewed my performance every quarter and the percentage of issues I developed on my subjects was only one of the many statistics with which I was measured. My percentage was always significantly above average. Still, they always pushed for more. Surprisingly, it would be this one measurement that would be the genesis for the unraveling of a great company in the near future. However, no one knew it at the time.

As my career progressed with USIS I eventually began conducting background security investigations for another one of their clients, the National Reconnaissance Office,lxx or NRO, a little-known intelligence agency of the U.S. government. The NRO was tasked with both designing and operating clandestine reconnaissance satellites. The government uses these secret spy satellites to gather intelligence on both enemy and friendly governments. The very existence of the

NRO, including the actual name of the organization, was classified until September of 1992.

I would find that the subjects associated with my NRO investigations represented the very cream of the crop. They rarely had any issues outside of an occasional speeding ticket. The work itself was highly compartmentalized. I was given a separate secure laptop with numerous layers of passwords and encryption just for these files. I flew to Fairfax, Virginia and received training in a nondescript building in a small office park about fifteen miles from the Pentagon. Details of the NRO investigations were top secret and, to maintain operational security, the investigations were referred to by USIS personnel as Air Force investigations or the Air Force contract. In fact, my initial training for the contract was conducted by a gentleman wearing an U.S. Air Force uniform, although his name wasn't provided to us nor did his uniform bear a name tag.

As the year continued on, the workload and pressure to produce results with USIS continued unabated. In my last year working for them it was not uncommon for me to drive over one hundred miles a day and work up to ten hours a day; often six days a week. The upside was that with all the overtime, I was making decent money for the first time in my life. However, I rarely had time to spend it. Huntsville was euphemistically referred to as a "one-person duty station" but I consistently carried the investigative workload of two or more people. Further evidenced by the fact that, once I left the company, USIS replaced me with two full-time investigators.

Of course, the frenetic work load was not just present in Huntsville. It was felt throughout the company. At the time, USIS was conducting approximately sixty-five percent of all U.S. government background investigations and being paid about $200 million a year in return. Competitors, such as CACI, Keypoint and MSM Security Services were always jostling for a bigger piece of the government pie. Given this type of pressure and deadline-driven atmosphere, it would be easy for investigators to cut corners to meet their prescribed goals. As it turns out, that's exactly what happened. Perhaps the company promised too much and expanded too quickly. In the end, USIS became a victim of its own success. I would end up leaving USIS in late 2001, long before these problems came to a head. They began with a whistle blower which led to an internal Department of Justice (DOJ) investigation. The situation was then further exacerbated by two seemingly unrelated incidents. Yet, these two isolated events within about four months of each other would garner the attention of a U.S. Senator and eventually lead to USIS losing the OPM contract.

The first incident involved a now infamous National Security Agency (NSA) contractor, code-named, *Citizen Four*. It took place in May 2013 when this Booz Allen Hamilton contractor named Edward Snowden, took a leave of absence from his position as a systems analyst for the NSA. Snowden walked out of the tunnel, a secret NSA facility[lxxi] in Hawaii where he worked and boarded a plane with stolen classified information. He told his supervisor he was flying back to the U.S. mainland for medical treatment, but he never arrived. Instead, he flew to Hong Kong and then eventually on to Moscow.

Edward Snowden was born June 21, 1983 in Elizabeth City, North Carolina, to Lonnie and Elizabeth Snowden. In May of 2004 he joined the U.S. Army Reserve and entered Special Forces training to become a Green Beret. He would be discharged four months later after breaking both legs in a training accident. Two years after that he joined the CIA and worked as a computer security specialist. He resigned in 2009 and then began working for Dell Computer and was contracted out to the NSA eventually landing at their facility in Ft. Meade, Maryland. It was there, shortly before his 2012 transfer to the Hawaii Regional Operations Center, that he first began stealing classified documents from the NSA and violating the Espionage Act of 1917. His final months were spent as a consultant for Booz Allen Hamilton before he turned over thousands of classified documents to Glenn Greenwald, a reporter for *The Guardian* and Laura Poitras, a documentary filmmaker.

Snowden stated that he revealed the classified information because he did not want to live in a society that spied on its citizens, as the NSA does. Veteran Academy award winning director Oliver Stone would go on to portray Snowden as a whistleblower turned hero in his 2016 film, Snowden. Stone mischaracterized the role and function of the NSA and elevated Snowden to a Jason-Bourne-like character. In reality, he was essentially a low-level contractor. I felt Stone's depiction was a bit heavy-handed as well.

The second event occurred four months later. On September 16, 2013 at 7:53 a.m., a U.S. Navy veteran and civilian contractor named Aaron Alexis arrived at the Washington Navy Yard on the banks of the Anacostia River in Washington, D.C. He had been working there on a joint Navy Marine Corps computer network for The Experts, a private information technology government contractor. After passing through the security check at the front gate and parking his car, Alexis calmly entered building 197. He carefully assembled a Remington 12-gauge tactical shotgun in a fourth-floor public restroom. He then exited and casually walked from room to room and floor to floor fatally shooting twelve people and wounding three. He then stole a Beretta 9mm semi-automatic handgun from a security officer whom he fatally shot. The shootings continued for about an hour and Alexis was stopped only when Washington, D.C. police officer Dorian DeSantis fatally shot Alexis in the head during a short gun fight.

As it turns out, Alexis had been suffering from mental illness and had been hearing voices. He believed he was being controlled by low frequency electromagnetic waves. He was also treated for severe insomnia on more than one occasion.

Interestingly, both Alexis and Snowden's security clearance investigations had been conducted by the same government contractor, USIS. That, in and of itself, is not peculiar. Most government security clearances were conducted by USIS. And to be fair, vetting an individual for a security clearance is no guarantee there won't be problems in the future. But with two high profile cases occurring within four months of each other, lawmakers began frothing at the mouth and looking for someone to blame.

What USIS didn't know at the time, what they couldn't know, was that the DOJ and OPM's Inspector General had already begun an internal investigation of the company in late July 2011. This investigation began when a USIS director of field work services by the name of Blake Percival filed a qui tam[lxxii] whistleblower lawsuit against the company after he was summarily fired. Percival's lawsuit stipulated that he was fired for refusing to go along with a practice called dumping. In investigator vernacular, to dump or flush background investigations is to categorize them as completed, when they in fact were not. Percival's lawsuit, along with Snowden and Alexis' actions, would combine to form a perfect storm against the company.

The government investigation soon discovered that some USIS investigators and mid-level managers had cut corners and falsified background reports to keep up with the company's strict deadlines. Missouri Senator Claire McCaskill stated "From Edward Snowden to Aaron Alexis, what's emerging is a pattern of failure on the part of this company…" That was a bit of an overstatement considering the fine work accomplished by the professional investigators at USIS. McCaskill was clearly preening for the cameras. Still, the DOJ investigation and Percival's whistleblower lawsuit were serious charges. The U.S. government ultimately sued USIS for 665,000 incomplete and otherwise unsatisfactory background investigations. Altegrity, USIS' parent company was forced to file for chapter 11 bankruptcy in 2015. As a result, all 2,500 background investigators and support personnel were summarily laid off. While Snowden and Alexis' actions brought undue attention to USIS, it was the internal investigation and resulting bankruptcy that would serve as the final nail in USIS' coffin.

On a personal level my experience working with USIS was initially very good. I often spoke with Phil Harper, the CEO, taking a generous helping of M&M's in his office. He kept them in a clear, glass candy dish on his desk. I was a brand-new investigator at the cave for training, but Harper had an open-door policy. He was willing to speak with anyone about the future of USIS. A former U.S. Army airborne infantry officer, he was long gone before USIS went south.

Like Harper, my district manager Wanda was a consummate professional. Indeed, all the people I met and worked with at USIS were outstanding. Much of the problems with USIS transpired long after I had left, and it had been acquired by a string of investors. I was just a single investigator in a one-man duty station; a small cog in a gigantic wheel. I was continually spread thin and overworked as I was pushed to meet impossible deadlines. Aside from wanting my own private investigation firm, that was my primary factor for leaving USIS.

In the end, what I experienced as an over-worked investigator was prescient considering what eventually happened to USIS. The relentless drive to uncover issues and to meet impossible deadlines led directly to the overall demise of USIS. Investigators were pushed to meet deadlines called CD's or critical dates to ensure that we kept the OPM contract. Some obviously began to cut corners under the strain. I wouldn't discount the influence of supervisors who pushed impossible deadlines at every level in the organization.

One last story about my time with USIS. It involved a gigantic cat named Captain Pancake. As part of the security clearance process I regularly spoke with landlords and neighbors. Not only did I verify that the subject resided at the location during the time frame indicated, I inquired as to what kind of tenant they were. On one of my last cases my subject had been a foster child and so I ended up speaking with his foster mother. She lived in a dilapidated mobile home in a small town in East Texas. It was a very hot and humid August day as she welcomed me into her home. I don't know if she was sick or just couldn't afford to run her air conditioner, but it was stifling hot inside the trailer. She motioned me to a chair at her dining room table.

As I was going through the required questions and conducting my interview, without warning a large cat suddenly jumped up on the table in front of me. It was a huge, twenty-five-pound Ragdoll house cat and he plopped down directly in front of me and sat and stared. I had never seen a cat as big as a dog. I paused my questioning, expecting the woman to shoo the cat from her dining room table, but she just smiled and said "Isn't she beautiful? Say hello to Captain Pancake." I sheepishly extended a greeting to the cat and then, despite the stifling heat and my new feline friend staring at me, continued my interview.

Moments later the cat began violently coughing and dry heaving in an attempt to cough up a hair ball right in front of me. I looked over again at the woman. In the intense heat of her home she was wearing a thick, white wool turtle neck sweater. She pulled a soft drink bottle to her lips to take a drink and I spotted several long cat hairs stuck to the spout of the bottle. She didn't seem to notice as she took a long swig. At that exact moment, the cat in front of me sneezed; and I mean really sneezed. It was so loud it sounded like a human sneezing. I looked over at Captain Pancake and saw her entire nose and mouth covered in cat mucous, which she then promptly began to lick clean. "That's it," I jumped up to leave. My stomach was starting to turn. Between the oppressive heat, Captain Pancake licking his mucous and the ubiquitous presence of cat hairs, I couldn't take any more. "Thank you for your time," I said, and then hurriedly walked out the door as fast as I could. I was picking cat hair off my suit for the rest of the day.

CHAPTER 11

THE MISSOURI COMPROMISE

On Tuesday, April 23, 2002, *The Fulton Sun*, the local newspaper in Fulton, Missouri carried the following story:

New Private Investigator Has an Eye for Crime

By Kimberly Long

"Sweltering in hot cars for long periods, peering at people from behind binoculars and occasionally having doors slammed in his face, are all in a day's work for Fulton's first-ever private "eye."

Scott Fulmer opened his private investigation firm last month called, Investigations Across Missouri, LLC. The Texas native admits it's not the most glamorous occupation, but it's one he enjoys doing and one that's in high demand in mid-Missouri.

While exploring possible locations for his business, Fulmer noticed that most private investigation services available to mid-Missouri residents were in Kansas City and St. Louis, which is one reason he chose Fulton as his home base.

"Instead of people having to pay the higher priced investigators we figured we could provide a professional organization in mid-Missouri that can handle all kinds of situations" Fulmer said. With his in-laws already living in Callaway County, Fulmer said "Fulton seemed the ideal place to settle down."

Being a private investigator is "not exactly" what television depicts, Fulmer said. *"I don't drive a Ferrari and I don't look like Tom Selleck,"* He said jokingly. *In reality, he said he's more like Jim Rockford of the "Rockford Files."*

"I spend a lot of time in my car, following trails and finding people. I've never been beaten up, but I have been chased by dogs before."

During his 10 years in the profession, Fulmer has conducted investigations in Missouri, Arkansas, Louisiana and Texas while working with U.S. Investigations – one of the largest private investigative firms in the United States.

His clientele have included the Drug Enforcement Agency (DEA), Immigration and Naturalization Services (INS), U.S. Customs, Border Patrol and Nuclear Power Plants. He's also investigated child abuse cases, worker's compensation and insurance fraud, located lost individuals and gathered divorce evidence.

"In this business, you have to be multifaceted," Fulmer explained. *He noted, having a good personality and being creative also helps. "You have to think fast on your feet and often times go with your gut feeling, because in most cases there's no one to ask questions of."*

With a bachelor's degree in criminal justice and resources from his previous investigating positions, Fulmer feels he's qualified to provide the type of services Fulton residents can use.

"We have partners in connection throughout the state that can give us a wider geographic reach," Fulmer noted. *With the selling point of a "Peace of mind when you absolutely have to know," Fulmer plans to focus his attention on domestic cases and doing work for attorneys, adjusters, insurance companies, small business, and workers' compensation cases,* he said.

Knowing the bad reputation that some private investigators have when it comes to costs and expenses, Fulmer said there are aspects that set him aside from the rest.

"We don't charge for expenses, just the flat rate and mileage," Fulmer said. "It's not just about the money. It's about helping people and having satisfaction about what you do. "Our goal is not to nickel and dime people to death."

Aside from private investigation, Fulmer also served four years with the U.S. Army during the Gulf War. He currently resides in Fulton with his wife Valerie, and their three children."

In late 2001 I resigned my position with USIS and moved my family from Huntsville to Fulton, Missouri, with plans to finally start my own private investigation firm. I have always had a desire to be a big fish in a small pond and a return to San Antonio would mean the opposite. Furthermore, my preference has always been to conduct a variety of investigations and not just a single type. Large markets like San Antonio require focus on a single type of investigation in order to be successful. Fulton was a small town situated in the center of the state; half way between St. Louis and Kansas City. Furthermore, Valerie's family lived there, and it would give my children and I a chance to spend some time getting to know them better. My mother-in-law, Linda gets a kick out of my line of work and always wants to hear about my latest cases and if I'm "packing heat." For the record, yes Linda. Always.

Despite the dreadful humidity, I had been happy living in Huntsville. We made some very good friends we still have to this day. I had originally pled with my managers at USIS to allow me to continue to work for them in Huntsville as a part-time contractor. This would have allowed me to form my own company and conduct other private investigations in the area while working for USIS. Wanda agreed, but Clyde Farnsworth, the USIS regional manager based in put the kibosh on that option. He took it as a personal affront that I would deign to leave the mighty USIS. Farnsworth was a retired U.S. Marine Lieutenant Colonel on his second career. To the Colonel, you just didn't abandon the team. I thought it would have been a win-win for everyone involved but Farnsworth saw it differently. And he called my bluff. So, I left. I've always had to live life on my own terms. In retrospect, it proved to be the best decision. Especially considering the eventual bankruptcy and sad demise of USIS.

Valerie and I had spent the first ten years of our marriage living near my family in San Antonio. We struck a compromise and decided to relocate to Missouri. We wanted our children to get to know her side of the family and I longed to live in an area with four seasons. So, in December of 2001 we packed up a large yellow Penske moving truck and drove the two days to Fulton, arriving late at night in a snow storm. Valerie's family was happy to see us. They all came out to help us load our belongings into a storage unit until we could find a place of our own.

Fulton is a small town of about thirteen thousand people and home to Westminster College. It was there, in March of 1945 shortly before World War Two ended, Winston Churchill gave his famous speech and coined the phrase "iron curtain." It was the smallest town I had ever lived in, but it was made better by the presence of Valerie's parents, siblings and their families.

Valerie is the oldest of five children with three brothers and a sister. Having no brothers of my own I was particularly interested in getting to know Valerie's. They were all wonderful. I seemed to get along best with her brother Todd. I would find Valerie's family to be some of the most friendly, caring and helpful people you could ever hope to meet.

At the time, Missouri was one of the few remaining states in the U.S. that did not have a state requirement for private investigators to be licensed. So, I became licensed through the City of Columbia, Missouri, about thirty minutes west of Fulton and home to the University of Missouri. Columbia was the county seat of Boone County and, with well over 100,000 people in the area, where I would be spending much of my time conducting investigations anyway. I hired a law firm to form an LLC and called my company Investigations Across Missouri. I rented a post office box and some telephone lines, and I was in business. Or so I thought.

Starting a private investigation firm, indeed, starting any kind of business venture from the ground floor is no easy task. Although there's no requirement for inventory or overhead, it does require clients, of which, I had none. Obviously, world domination was going to take a while longer. In the meantime, to support my family I began working part-time as a paralegal investigator for the appellate division of the Missouri State Public Defender System. I worked out of their Columbia office in a business park on West Nifong Street. All our clients had been found guilty at the trial level and were currently incarcerated in several Missouri state prisons in the surrounding area. I assisted their attorneys as the inmates filed appeals. We represented the indigent; those who were in trouble with the law but could not afford an attorney. I worked with these public defenders as we took a second look at their conviction, re-interviewing witnesses, looking at evidence and making certain that the law had been followed correctly.

Despite what you may have heard about public defenders, the men and women I worked with were fine attorneys. They cared very deeply about justice and due process. They were experienced and worked hard to represent their clients, even though most of them were guilty. Still, even guilty people deserve an attorney. Especially guilty people. My boss Steve Harris was head of the appellate division. He was an exceptional attorney and a real pleasure to work for.

The cases I worked ran the whole gamut from murder to assault, rape, robbery and drug possession. They often went from the sublime to the ridiculous. I recall a case where a couple of friends, Hank and Jack had been repairing a car at Hank's house. Phillip, an acquaintance of Hank's, arrived to assist in the car repairs. Phillip arrived clutching a cold six-pack of beer because, "Beer is the perfect addition to frustrating car repairs." About an hour and a half into the repairs Phillip stepped inside Hank's house to grab beer number four. However, when he opened the refrigerator door he found the carton devoid of beer. Irritated, he walked back outside and confronted Hank and Jack about who had taken the last beer. When Jack admitted he had, Phillip reached into his waistband, grabbed a 9mm handgun and shot Jack dead. Over a beer.

During my investigation, I found out that a distant relative of Jack's had been on the original jury trial that convicted Phillip. Phillip was guilty. He was a contemptible human being who shot a man for drinking the last beer. But like everyone else he was entitled to a fair trial. The rules must apply to everyone, even to someone like Phillip. Especially to someone like Phillip, or they mean nothing at all.

CONFESSIONS OF A PRIVATE EYE

I spent my mornings working for the public defender and private investigator trying to build up my business. Due to t much of central Missouri, I often found myself traveling to St. investigations for my own company. It was there in Webster (.., ... upper income neighborhood west of downtown St. Louis, in which I first saw the hands of Joy.

Joy resided in a gorgeous, two-story, red brick home surrounded by red maple trees not far from Blackburn Park. She was a tall woman with short red hair and very fair skin. Her husband Deke was the special agent in charge of the St. Louis division of the Drug Enforcement Administration (DEA). Deke was responsible for enforcing the Controlled Substances Act. On the other hand, Joy spent her days committing insurance fraud. Knowing who her husband was, I began the case with a little trepidation. I would have to be very careful, not only because they lived in an upper income neighborhood, but because I anticipated Joy to be surveillance savvy.

On a hot and humid July morning, I began surveillance near Joy's home. She had previously been involved in a car accident and had allegedly injured her back and both her hands. But the claims adjuster handling her case thought something smelled fishy about Joy's claim.

It didn't take very long to get the goods on Joy. I found out where she was planning on going each day and what her plans were. I wish I could tell you how I found out, but to do so would reveal confidential sources and methods. Suffice it to say that despite Deke's position in the DEA, he had a real operational security problem at home. As fast as you can say Deus ex Machina[lxxiii] I was able to some academy award winning video of Joy doing her thing, including lots of activity with her bending over and extensive use of her hands. The only thing alleged about Joy was her honesty.

For starters, Joy was attached to her cell phone like it was a natural appurtenance coming out of her ear. Throughout the investigation I never saw her without the phone. Ever. She drove with the phone pressed to her ear. She walked around with the phone pressed to her ear. She dragged the trash can to the curb with the phone pressed to her ear. In all the activity of her which I recorded, she always had the phone pressed to her left ear. I don't know who she was talking to, but it must've been important. As a result, she was more interested in the phone calls than anything else going on around her. At the time cell phones had really begun to take off and they were somewhat of a status symbol. People brandished them in public all the while carrying on unimportant conversations. I could've sat naked in a lawn chair holding sparklers and videotaping her from the top of my surveillance vehicle and she wouldn't have noticed.

I began following Joy all over the city videotaping her every move. The pièce de résistance occurred late in the afternoon on my last day of surveillance. Joy pulled up to a kiosk outside a grocery store which dispensed filtered water. I videotaped her as she got out of the car, raised the hatchback and began to fill eight five-gallon plastic jugs with water. She filled each one up, capped it, and then struggled to put it back in the car. It's no wonder she struggled. I found out later that a full jug weighed about 40 pounds. This was not an activity for someone with a back and hand injury. I guess all those phone conversations had made her thirsty. The real miracle was that even as she struggled to carry those 40-pound jugs of water and place them into her car, she still managed to keep her cell phone pressed to her ear with her shoulder. This woman had talent. The result was that Joy was fine. There was nothing wrong with her hands or her back. The only malady Joy suffered from was an acute case of dishonesty and greed. She exaggerated her claim because she wanted to collect a larger insurance settlement.

I continued working to build my private investigation company in Missouri, but my efforts were painstakingly slow and met with mixed results. Building any business takes time but everything seemed to be moving at a glacial pace for Investigations Across Missouri. That said, some work did trickle in. Unlike my position with the Missouri public defender, not all my investigations involved serious crimes. One of my first cases involved a dog named Neville.

It might surprise you to learn that about a third of homeowner liability claims involve dog bites. My client stated he had been bitten by a vicious Pitbull named Neville while he was strolling down the public sidewalk minding his own business. Neville's owners, on the other hand, said my client had taunted the dog, thus, the client got what he deserved. I did some investigating and discovered that Neville was indeed a problem. I gathered statements from neighbors who said the dog was treated poorly by his owners and often escaped to terrorize the neighborhood. Furthermore, I found numerous animal control complaints including three other dog bites Neville was responsible for within the last seven years. John Grogan, journalist and author of *Marley and Me*, once said, "There's no such thing as a bad dog, just a bad owner."[lxxiv] This was certainly true in Neville's case. The evidence I obtained would help my client win his claim against Neville's irresponsible owners.

Not all dogs I've encountered on my investigations were vicious like Neville. I once followed a lanky construction worker named Bruce who had filed a personal injury claim after an automobile accident. Due to his severe injuries, he was unable to work. Imagine my surprise when Bruce loaded up his old dilapidated truck with personal tools and left his Jefferson City, Missouri home shortly after 5:00 AM one morning. I followed him south on state highway 54 until he arrived in Osage Beach, Missouri. He turned off the highway and continued east into a wooded area near the Lake of the Ozarks, a large 54,000-acre lake that wound its way through the woods. Bruce eventually turned onto a narrow dirt road. I slowly applied the brakes until he was about a half a mile ahead of me. Eventually I came around a corner and saw his yellow truck parked next to several other vehicles on the side of the road. I arrived in time to catch a brief glimpse of him. He was descending a steep wooden staircase down into the woods where a home was being built next to the lake. I could hear the sounds of a power saw and hammering but due to the thick woods I couldn't see a thing. I grabbed my video camera and my desert camouflage boonie hat from the Gulf War and left the road above. I slowly descended the hill down into the woods just west of the wooden staircase. It was steep, and I found myself having to grasp several trees just to keep my balance. Once I descended to the bottom of the hill close to the lake I began moving forward towards the sounds of the construction. It was necessary for me to get close enough so I could observe Bruce working on the home. I moved into a prone position laying on the cool leaves. As I lay in the thick woods on the edge of the property I could see the house in front of me. The huge lake was on my left and the hill I had just descended was on my right. In between the sounds of the hammering and the power tools I could hear the water from the lake as it gently lapped against the banks. Somewhere in the distance I heard the faint sound of a jet ski. I momentarily closed my eyes and considered taking a nap. The weather was perfect. Rays of sunshine streamed through the thick canopy of trees overhead. I was reminded of my time at the U.S. Army Jungle Survival School in Panama. I could definitely get used to living here, I thought.

I could observe about seven men, including my subject, working on the house. A black and white border collie sat lazily watching them. I began shooting video of Bruce as he hammered away and involved himself in various other physical activities that belied his severe car injuries. What I didn't know was that in the meantime the dog had taken notice of me. Evidently one of the 300 million olfactory receptors in the dog's nose must have caught my scent. In a moment, he was standing next to me. My first thought was that my surveillance was going to be burned. And then I was going to be mauled by a border collie. That's when the dog reached down and licked my hand. He turned out to be very friendly. He then laid down next to me and joined me in my surveillance for a short while. I reached over and stroked the coat of my new friend and whispered, "go back." Surprisingly, the dog obeyed. He slowly sauntered back over to the home and sat down in his original spot. As I continued to shoot video that morning, the dog occasionally picked his head up and looked in my direction. He would then turn back to the house and lay his head down on his front paws as if he was preserving our little secret. Meanwhile, I gathered enough video of Bruce to prove his injuries were minor.

Many of the investigations I've conducted have been heartbreaking. I was given a workers' compensation case in Chesterfield, Missouri that involved a police officer. We expect police officers to be honest, and I sincerely believe most are. But every occupation has their problem employees, even law enforcement. Tim Rooney was a patrol officer who had injured his back attempting to subdue a suspect. Rooney was well-respected and mid-way through his career, having been on the force for about ten years. In accordance with procedures, he was placed on workers' compensation and required to attend physical therapy. However, over time the claims adjuster assigned to his case noticed certain red flags popping up. Tim often missed his medical appointments. Whenever the adjuster called, he never answered his telephone. A city employee who knew Tim saw him lifting weights at a local gym. So, the adjuster decided to assign surveillance to find out what he was up to. Tim's file was given to me and I broke the case on the first weekend.

I began surveillance on a warm Saturday morning in his neighborhood. His house was the first one on the block, on the corner of a very busy road. As it turned out, I didn't' have to wait too long to catch Tim in action. After about two hours of inactivity I watched as he suddenly appeared on the side his house. He had come from the backyard and was pushing a blue wheel barrow full of an assortment of gardening and landscaping tools. As tiny beads of sweat rolled down the back of my neck I obtained video of him using a shovel to clean out a flower bed. I thought I had obtained good video of him until I watched him walk over to the side of his house and begin using a post hole digger. He was evidently replacing a section of fence. I continued shooting video as he rammed the post hole digger into the ground with tremendous force. He then moved the two hardwood handles back and forth to dig out a hole for a fence post. I don't know if you've ever used a post hole digger, but if you do I promise you, you'll find muscles you never knew you had. I believed the video of him using the post hole digger was really good, but then Tim surprised me again. He walked back to the wheel barrow and this time pulled out a pick axe. He began using the pick axe for the better part of the morning on rocks in and around the flower bed. After almost three hours of video on Tim I started my car and quietly drove away in the direction of my office. I completed my report and submitted it, along with my video and invoice. I don't know what became of Tim. Unless the case ends up in court I rarely hear about the final results. But I do know that he exaggerated his claim like so many others. Tim was actually in very good shape. And he had a great work ethic. At least when it came to lawn maintenance.

Investigations involving children are the most difficult to deal with. One case in Missouri involved an attorney who turned out to be a pedophile. When it comes to evil in the world, there's a tendency to consider the extreme examples of people like Adolf Hitler and Osama Bin Laden. And yes, those guys were evil. But we often fail to consider that evil resides in our own neighborhoods, stands next to us in line at the grocery store or serves with us on the PTA. Sometimes the worst examples of evil are people who look and act in ways we consider normal.

This case involved a low-level drug dealer in the aforementioned Osage Beach area who went by the sobriquet, Flip. For some reason, he owed his lawyer a great deal of money but didn't have the money to pay him. I guess even drug dealers are broke sometimes. Instead, Flip sent his thirteen-year-old daughter

Grace to the lawyer's house overlooking the Lake of the Ozarks to have sex with him. For the entire weekend. Cases such as these are difficult to stomach. I try not to even think about them. But I do believe there's a special place in Hell for people like that.

CHAPTER 12

YOU MAY ALL GO TO HELL AND I WILL GO TO TEXAS

Like many things in life, my private investigation business in Missouri did not work out as I had planned. I can tell you that self-employment is not for the faint of heart. There were several reasons for the setback including family pressures and a lack of cash flow. I was on a shoe-string budget. I had to work my public defender job during the day to support my family. This left me precious little time to find both new customers for my own business and then do the actual work. It all boiled down to the one reason most businesses fail: lack of customers. I didn't know it at the time, but I would start and fail at several other private investigation companies over the next decade. It wasn't until my move to Salt Lake City, where I started Fulmer, P.I., that I would ultimately find longstanding success.

For now, I packed up yet another truck and moved my family back to San Antonio in the Summer of 2002. I found myself working for Mike Farmer again. He gladly welcomed back the Fulmer Luck and I hit the ground running. My dream of being a self-employed private eye was going to take a little bit longer. Until then, I sunk my teeth into work.

I continued working both workers' compensation and liability investigations. One of the first cases I worked on my return to Texas involved a single mother of three I dubbed the Mother of Roller Coasters. I traveled back to Arlington, Texas where I had lived when I first began working for USIS. Except this time, I was setting up a surveillance on Blair Hansen, a single mother of three with an injured back.

It's been said that X marks the spot; that if you dig you'll find buried treasure. But private investigative work is not that easy. In fact, despite what you see on television it is often rare to find a blatant smoking gun. Like the proverbial pot of gold at the end of the rainbow, definitive results can be and often are elusive. I deal primarily in preponderance of evidence or shades of grey. This is especially true with workers' compensation surveillance. Gathering film of a subject claiming to have a bad back as she is bending over to pick up her crying baby may seem like great video. But what else is she supposed to do? When it comes to workers' compensation fraud you also want video of the subject being active on more than one day. You want film showing a range of various activities over time. Sometimes you get lucky and obtain great video that speaks volumes. If a picture is worth a thousand words, then video must be worth a million.

And that's what happened with Blair. She was about medium height with a nice figure. She had long, straight, brunette hair and a fondness for wearing snakeskin patterned pants. Despite being pretty, she seemed to have a permanent scowl on her face for some reason. Perhaps it was because she was a single mother with three children under the age of five. That certainly couldn't be easy. Maybe she was just unhappy. Either way, I had already conducted surveillance on her for several days without much luck. It was time for a different tactic. So that's when I decided to take Blair's garbage.

I instituted what we call in the private investigation business a "trash pull." In other words, I went dumpster diving. Blair lived with her three children in a white brick four-plex in a neighborhood east of S. Cooper Street on the southcentral side of Arlington. She had an assigned trash can which made my job easier, but no less disgusting. I discovered her trash pickup was twice a week in the early mornings. I showed up near Blair's apartment at 2:00 AM one cool September morning and, before you can say California v. Greenwood,lxxv I had grabbed her trash, thrown it in the trunk of my car and sped away.

After making sure no one was tailing me I returned home and spread out a thick plastic groundsheet on my garage floor. I sprinkled baby powder on my hands and then slipped them into a pair of blue latex gloves. I then carefully emptied Blair's trash out on the groundsheet. You can learn a lot about people by going through their trash. Maybe more than you really want to know. I discovered what type of medications Blair was taking and what pharmacy filled them. I found out who her doctor was. I found used condoms and cigarette butts with lipstick on them. I discovered what brand of sanitary napkins she favored. A veritable DNA goldmine. I learned she preferred Sensodyne toothpaste and unhealthy microwavable food. I was looking for something; for anything that would give me an edge in my investigation.

I eventually found it. Among the empty soup cans and the Final Net Hairspray I discovered a receipt and a note. It was a receipt for several tickets to Six Flags over Texas, an amusement park in north Arlington near Interstate Highway 30. There was also a handwritten note that said, *"Bridgett said Friday is best. Will meet at your place at 9:00 AM."* I had apparently stumbled upon a discarded phone message from Blair's babysitter. I learned that Blair and her posse would be

Six Flags on Friday. So, I went and bought myself a ticket and then returned Friday morning to Blair's house shortly before 9:00 AM.

I was only twenty minutes into the surveillance when Blair's friend Bridgette, another single mother, arrived with her children. A half an hour after that and everyone was loaded up and we were on our way to Six Flags. It's wonderful following someone on a moving surveillance when you know where they're going. It certainly makes the job easier. Even so, my adrenal glands were pumping on overload. We arrived at Six Flags and found a parking spot. I got video as Blair and her party unloaded the vehicle and entered the park. She and Bridgett had a total of five children of various ages in tow. It was at this point that my surveillance skills really came into play. Six Flags is a large amusement park sitting on over 200 acres. I had to be close enough to get video of Blair, but far enough away for her not to notice the middle-aged white man with a video camera who seemed to be watching her every move. I brought a backpack with hats and extra shirts should I need to alter my appearance. With several small children in tow they didn't walk very fast. But even if they had, Blair's distinctive snake skin pants were easy to spot.

Six Flags had 13 roller coasters. And Blair rode every one of them. She rode a few more than once. Fortunately, the park was not very crowded, so the lines moved rather quickly. Once she got in line I found a park bench and sat and waited until she finally got on the ride. Then I pulled out my video camera. On every one of the roller coasters she held her arms up high above her head and screamed at the top of her lungs. I captured it all in vivid digital color. The jerks, the jolts and the upside-down loops couldn't have been good for her alleged back injury. Still, she didn't seem to exhibit any pain or discomfort that I c exited each ride as if she was walking out of the theater after a good n didn't seem to be anything wrong with Blair's back. I passed the vide claims adjuster who was ecstatic. The mother of roller coasters had made one mother of a mistake.

I continued to travel for work with Mike Farmer, conducting investigations throughout central and south Texas. Many of my subjects, like Blair, could be found participating in leisure or outdoor activities. Sometimes I got lucky and arrived at exactly the right moment. Like the fellow in Seguin, Texas who was mowing his lawn as I drove up. He smiled and waved at me and I smiled and waved back as if I lived in the neighborhood. I then circled the block and carefully set up in the parking lot of a duplex next to his home. I spent the next hour shooting video of him mowing, trimming, edging, raking and doing every other imaginable activity that was outside the scope of his alleged injury. And then there was Mitch Brady. He just sat in his boat. In the driveway.

Pouring out of Canyon Lake, the Guadalupe River winds its way through the beautiful Texas Hill Country and past the city of New Braunfels, first settled by German immigrants in 1845. Beginning in December of each year, the Texas Parks and Wildlife Department stock areas of the Guadalupe River, just below Canyon Dam, with Rainbow Trout. As you drive northwest from New Braunfels on highway 306 near the intersection of Highway 2673 you begin to see several cars parked intermittently on the side of the road, empty of any occupants. Between December and March of each year this area of the river is a favorite for fly fishing. I have driven by several times in December in the cool early morning hours just as

The sun rises and begins to glisten on the cold fast-moving water. There is always a lone figure standing in the river like a silent centurion preserving the age-old tradition of fly fishing. All you can hear is the rushing and babbling of the water and then suddenly the centurion moves. With an explosive backward snap of the wrist he casts his line...an artificial fly at the end of a fly line comes barreling across the surface of the water like an insect. It was in this same location in which Mitchell "Mitch" Brady liked to fish, often two to three times a week. That is until Mitch suffered a shoulder injury at work and was placed on workers comp.

Mitch's injury was so serious it appeared that he might even need surgery. However, just as in the case of Tim Rooney, the police officer from Missouri, certain red flags began to pop up that made the adjuster question the legitimacy of Mitch's claim. Among them, he never answered the phone when the adjuster called. His wife always said he was sleeping and couldn't be disturbed. And he missed several of his physical therapy appointments.

The claims adjuster happened to know that Mitch liked to fish. There was no doubt in her mind he would go fishing on the weekend. This activity would make for great video, especially in light of his shoulder injury. The adjuster called Mike and Mike called me. I pulled out of the driveway at about 4:00 AM and turned my surveillance vehicle towards Mitch's house on the south side of San Antonio near S. Presa road. One needs to get up early to catch someone going fishing.

It was Saturday morning and Mitch's neighborhood was quiet. It seemed everyone was either still asleep or out of town. Everyone, that is, except Mitch. He was in a bathrobe sitting in his small aluminum fishing boat which was parked on a boat trailer underneath his car port. He was fiddling with fishing equipment and I assumed I had hit pay dirt. Mitch was going fishing. Or so I thought he didn't go fishing that day nor did he go fishing the next day. But it didn't matter. Because what he did do was worth my surveillance efforts. Apparently, Mitch had purchased a new fishing rod, because from about 8:00 am until 10:00 am Saturday morning I obtained video of him standing in the street as he practiced casting his line. For two hours straight, with all the strength he could muster, Mitch practiced casting the line. He used his right arm (and shoulder) which he had allegedly injured at work. He cast his right arm back in an arch and then punched it forward releasing the mono-filament line. He then used his right hand to reel the line back in. He cast it sideways and reeled it in. He cast it overhead, from the left, from the right, again and again. Anyone with a healthy arm and shoulder would've been exhausted in short order, but especially someone who supposedly had suffered a shoulder injury. But still, Mitch persisted. The adjuster was right. He did like to fish.

The crazy thing was he did all his casting directly underneath a power line. I half expected him to latch onto a live power line and fry himself, but it never happened. I recorded all his movements in crisp digital color and presented the video to the adjuster. I had reeled in a fresh case of fraud and put the kibosh on Mitch's workers comp benefits. The only fishing Mitch was going to be doing in the future was fishing for another job.

I'm often asked what it's like being a private investigator. Truthfully, it can be quite boring at times, but it has its moments. Each day is different. With regards to domestic-related cases, people come to you with serious problems. Many are in deep emotional distress over issues having to do with their marriage, children, finances or their business. Some of their issues are out-right unpleasant. I've dealt with kidnappings, child abduction, assault and domestic abuse. I once had a Hell's Angel biker realize he was under surveillance. He took off after me in his apartment complex in Austin, but I was able to get away. I've interviewed rapists in prison who admitted to their vulgar deeds, individuals who were sexually molested as children and a few other things that I don't wish to write about.

You can eventually find yourself getting past the point where you are surprised by the kinds of things you encounter. You find yourself constantly having to come up with last-minute, solutions for your client's often self-inflicted problems. Then there's the weird and the wacky stuff. I remember one guy called and said the government was watching him. He had placed aluminum foil over all his windows. Still, every time he left his home he noticed airplanes and helicopters flying overhead, watching his every move. Wherever he went, the airplanes and helicopters followed him. He asked if I could conduct aviation surveillance and see who was watching him. I convinced him his request was not financially feasible.

I had a woman call from Karnes City, Texas. She said she was in the U.S. Marshals Service's Witness Security program and was hiding from organized crime. She had reason to believe the mafia was aware of her location. She asked me to help her move her residence before they found her and killed her. I figured if that was the case then certainly the Marshals would've moved her. In the end, I didn't find her credible.

On another occasion, I was in San Antonio near the intersection of N. Walters and E. Houston street working a trademark infringement investigation. As I sat there I happened to notice an older prostitute walking up and down the street plying her trade. Throughout the morning, she was picked up by numerous a variety of cars, only to be dropped off a short time later. After a couple of hours of this I noticed she didn't look very well. As I watched her walk across the road she suddenly stopped in the middle of the street. She placed her right hand on her stomach, then suddenly bent forward and projectile vomited, violently emptying the contents of her stomach onto the busy street. No one came to her aid. Cars continued to pass her by. I felt very badly for her, but I couldn't break my surveillance to render her assistance. A short time later I saw her get picked up by yet another customer.

I've accomplished a lot of surveillance out in rural areas which can be very difficult. It's usually impossible to set up a decent surveillance position with a clear view of the subject's house without raising suspicion. I once knew a private investigator who would sit on the side of the road with his car hood up pretending he had engine trouble. The problem with that little scenario is that folks in the country are usually very helpful. Everyone, including the subject, would stop by and ask if he needed assistance. With rural surveillance, I'm often forced to take what we call an indirect approach. This means I'm often a mile or two down the road waiting for the subject's vehicle to drive by, so I can pull in behind them.

Speaking of rural areas, a woman named Adeline called me from Ft. Stockton, Texas once. She told me she heard voices in her apartment. The voices used foul language and had begun to threaten her. She happened to sound very believable. But when she told me she also heard the voices in her neighborhood as she walked the dog I realized it was a mental health issue. The mental health cases can be the most difficult to decipher. But I always listen to potential clients and try to help at least in some small way. And then there was Doug Wheatley and a little case I call the Adventure of the Naked Baker.

Doug could not play nicely with others. Doug had no respect for women. Doug was a misanthrope. Doug worked as a baker for DeScansar, a luxury, four-star resort, just north of San Antonio. As a retirement gift for a parting female co-worker, he baked a chocolate cake with cream icing. The cake was in the exact shape of a certain part of the male anatomy. Did I mention Doug was a cretin? Not surprisingly, neither the female co-worker, nor resort management, were impressed. In fact, the woman filed a sexual harassment complaint. It seems that Doug had done this kind of thing before and possessed a generally chauvinistic attitude towards the opposite sex. Doug didn't know it at the time, but his little pastry penis project was the final straw for this prickly purveyor of perversion. He would be fired by the end of the week.

The resort contacted me because they wanted to conduct surveillance on Doug on a Friday, the day he was to be fired, as well as the remainder of that weekend. He had shown himself to be unpredictable and somewhat of a loose cannon. They wanted to make sure that after he was fired he didn't come back to work and cause problems or do something violent. This is, in fact, a common service provided by private eyes. It wasn't the first time, nor would it be the last time I would conduct surveillance on a terminated employee.

The resort management provided me background information on Doug, as well as a picture taken for his employee identification badge. When Friday morning arrived, I was in place at Doug's apartment complex at about 4:00 AM. I was dog-tired. It felt like someone had poured sand in my eyes. Doug was known to leave for work rather early which necessitated my even earlier than normal arrival. I found a suitable surveillance position in the parking lot of an adjacent apartment complex. The parking lot was about two feet higher than Doug's, thus, giving me a clear unobstructed view of his apartment, including his sliding glass doors. It was a view which, as it turned out, would present me with much more than I was prepared to see.

After about thirty minutes into the surveillance I saw a figure walking back and forth behind the sliding glass door. I picked up my video camera and zoomed in on what appeared to be Doug. But something was terribly wrong. He didn't look right. I initially thought he was wearing a pale white unitard. The irony is even that didn't surprise me. But unfortunately, that was not the case. As I sat contemplating why he would be wearing a white unitard, I suddenly had a moment of clarity. It was not a unitard. It was Doug. And he was naked. As a jay bird. Like the day he was born. Moreover, Doug was a pasty white old man who had stopped working out years ago.

It's one of the perils of the job, I suppose. Some things can't be unseen. You can't pour enough bleach in my eyes to help me forget the sight of a naked 60-year-old man. But it suggested a lesson every private investigator should know about reasonable expectation of privacy.

I followed Doug to work that morning all the while knowing what his eventual fate would be. As expected, he was fired. I watched him walk back out to his car a couple of hours after arriving. He was carrying a white cardboard banker's box with his personal belongings. I almost felt sorry for him. Almost. He returned home, and the rest of the weekend was uneventful. Other than a short trip to the grocery store and to rent a movie, he remained at home. Doug may have been a weirdo, but fortunately, he wasn't a violent weirdo.

As with most of my cases I try to learn something from every experience. When I saw Doug walking naked in his apartment I didn't shoot video of him. Yes, the curtains were wide open but even Doug the naked baker was entitled to a measure of privacy in his own home. And so it is with surveillance. I'm not a lawyer, but the term 'reasonable expectation of privacy' can be defined as a certain expectation of privacy recognized by normal society, whatever "normal" is. For example, I wouldn't put my camera over a privacy fence to videotape the subject. Nor would I come back at night and trim the subject's hedges because they were blocking my surveillance view of his front yard during the day time. It's a fine line and there are many gray areas in this business. Some things are illegal, while other things are legal but unethical.

In the summer of 2006 I would leave Mike Farmer's company for the second time and this time it would be for good. As you can imagine, he wasn't as excited about my leaving this time. Other than my brief foray in self-employment in Missouri, I had spent the better part of the last decade working for someone else. It was time to make my dream of self-employment a permanent reality. I became licensed in Texas and named my company Confidential Options. However, for some reason, my company was accidently listed under Family Planning in one of the many local yellow pages. I'm not sure how that happened, but as a result, I often received phone calls about performing abortions. I had to explain we didn't offer that particular service.

CHAPTER 13

SHE'S A LITTLE RUNAWAY

There was a great number of private investigators in San Antonio and throughout South Texas. Perhaps too many. Like Investigations Across Missouri, Confidential Options proved painfully slow to take off. During the course of marketing my business, I remembered a former client of Mike Farmers. Mike and the client had a falling out. As a result, we hadn't done any investigative work for them for almost a full year prior to the time I left to start my own firm. They were a large public utility that needed workers compensation investigations on a monthly basis. I thought about contacting them, but I was hesitant at first. I hadn't signed a non-compete agreement with Mike. Still, I didn't want to burn any bridges or be seen as stealing someone's clients. In the end however, I decided to at least stop in and say hello. I figured if they had a need they would tell me. As it turned out, they did. And I walked out thirty minutes later with my first client and two new cases. And with that, Confidential Options hit the ground running.

Aside from workers' compensation investigations, I have spent much of my 30 years as a private investigator working on what I call the trifecta: missing persons, runaways and kidnappings.

I was once retained by Randy Everett, a man from Boerne, Texas. He wanted to find his ex-girlfriend, Morgan. She had disappeared about a year prior after an argument. He just wanted to know if she was okay. It sounded simple enough. But things are never as simple as they seem in the private investigation business.

When it comes to finding missing persons, one must exercise caution. The person may not really be missing. They may have left due to abuse or because they were afraid. The client may be trying to stalk them. With domestic clients, I operate under the assumption that I'm only getting about half the story to begin with. And probably the half I am getting is peppered with some measure of lies and exaggerations. Such was the case with Randy.

After further conversations, he admitted to being verbally and physically abusive to Morgan. During one of our telephone conversations he jokingly said when he found out who she was with now, he was going to "murder the man." He then chuckled. Upon hearing that, the hairs on the back of my neck stood straight up. I asked if he was joking. "Of course," he said, with no emotion in his response. I wasn't convinced. Too many warning bells were going off. The last straw was when he admitted that he and Morgan had often laid in bed and talked about murdering Morgan's ex-husband, Dwight. I eventually refunded his retainer and told him I didn't feel comfortable moving forward with the case. I then quickly sent an email warning all the other private investigators in the South Texas area about Randy, just in case he tried to contact someone else. Then there was the guy who did kill his wife.

One of my first big cases involved trying to find a runaway in San Antonio. A commercial pilot by the name of Grant Perry lost his wife Ashley when she apparently drowned in the swimming pool of their Alamo Heights home.lxxvi

Located several miles north of downtown San Antonio, Alamo Heights is a small city with a population of about 7,000 and a median income of almost $100,000.00 per family. It is home to many of the old money families of San

Antonio. Barely two square miles, it's surrounded on all sides by San Antonio. The Perry's lived with their 16-year-old son Frederick in a beautiful Spanish Colonial home of white stucco protected by a canopy of large oak trees and a red terra cotta roof. Their home was on Patterson Avenue, not far from the Argyle Club, a private dinner club for the city's elites.

Initially, the incident did not attract much attention outside of South Texas. The Bexar County medical examiner ruled Ashley's death an accidental drowning, although, she had an elevated amount of diazepam in her system and a small gash on her head. He stated the gash was more than likely due to hitting her head on the pool. He suggested she had apparently taken too much diazepam and drowned in the pool. It sounded simple enough. Her husband Grant stated that she often forgot whether or not she had taken her meds and she may have doubled her dose, not realizing she had already taken the pills. Grant had an alibi, as he was visiting his mother in a nursing home at the time. The case was closed.

In his epic novel, *Anna Karenina*, author Leo Tolstoy wrote, "*All happy families are alike; each unhappy family is unhappy in its own way.*"lxxvii This proved to be the case with Grant and Ashley Perry. It would take time, but eventually the dark secrets of Grant Perry would find the light of day. It began with the Perry's oldest daughter, Charlotte. She had long harbored suspicions about her father. She and her mother were best friends and regular shopping partners. Once, on a shopping spree at the Shops at La Cantera on the far north side of San Antonio, Ashley told Charlotte that if anything ever happened to her they should look at Grant. After her mother's death, she began to consider foul play. It was Charlotte who discovered her father was having an affair with a San Antonio realtor named Penny on. She then began to suspect that her father may have had something her mother's death.

Due to Charlotte's persistent efforts, the case was eventually reopened, and authorities were able to prove that Grant had held his drugged wife down in the shallow end of the swimming pool and murdered her. Grant's alibi fell apart when one of the caregivers at his mother's nursing home adjusted the time line as to when Grant was there. Penny testified at the trial that he wanted to get rid of his wife.

With his mother dead and father in jail, Frederick went to live with his sister, Charlotte. Before this, it was Freddy, as he was called, who first found his mother's body in the swimming pool. Due to the trauma of discovering his mother's body and eventually learning his father was responsible, Freddy began suffering with depression. Charlotte would go on to spend thousands of dollars on therapy and counseling to help him. However, one night he snuck out of his bedroom window and disappeared into the night. Charlotte's sister Miranda called me from Portland, Oregon and asked if I could meet with Charlotte and help find Freddy. I was on an investigation in Coeur d'Alene, Idaho at the time, but I eventually met with Charlotte upon my return to San Antonio. She gave me pictures and other information on Freddy and then wrote a check for my fee. I found him in exactly 48 hours.

Finding a runaway is like trying to find a needle in a haystack. Young people don't leave the kinds of clues and footprints that adults do. They don't own homes or businesses and rarely own cars. But they all have cell phones and they're all engaged in social media. I eventually found Freddy living with a girl he had known at Alamo Heights High School. Her name was Gemma and they were living together in her bedroom in her mother's home. We later discovered that Freddy had told Gemma's mother that Charlotte and her husband Bruce had been verbally and emotionally abusive to him. Gemma's mother figured he was almost 17-years-old, so she let him stay.

I set up surveillance in the neighborhood but other than Gemma's mother and brother coming and going, it was a week before I saw Freddy. He was hiding out and keeping a low profile. But I knew he couldn't stand to be cooped up in the house forever. On a rainy Saturday afternoon, the garage door automatically opened, and a silver-colored sedan departed. I observed Gemma driving and an unknown male in the passenger seat. I followed them to a McDonald's drive-through and then a gas station where Gemma filled the vehicle up. I was able to zoom my video camera in and observe Freddy sitting in the car eating a burger. He had cut his normally long hair to alter his appearance, but it was definitely him.

After they returned to the house I telephoned the client. Charlotte was happy I had located Freddy but didn't want us to call the authorities just yet. She was in the middle of deciding on yet another out-of-state, in-patient clinic for Freddy; a place where he could get the help he needed. I closed the case and moved on. There were plenty of other people who needed my help. People like Fitzgerald Brooks.

The client told me Mr. Brooks "…disappears about 9:00 or 10:00 p.m. and then usually reappears the next morning. Sometimes he's gone for a couple of days." I was on an investigation in Omaha, Nebraska when I got a call about the weekly disappearance of Fitzgerald Brooks. Meghan Vernon was Fitz's sister and told me that he suffered from mental illness. He had been diagnosed with Schizophrenia but was able to live on his own due to a sizable family trust.

When he wasn't lounging at his Uvalde, Texas home Fitz spent his days wandering downtown on foot and smoking cigarettes nonstop. He frequented the same three restaurants for breakfast, lunch and dinner each day, often ordering the same menu item prepared in exactly the same way. He received his medication and a small cash allowance each evening from Juan Rodriguez, a home health nurse hired by the family. And then he began to disappear.

"We're worried about him," Meghan said. "We want you to follow him and find out where he goes and what he's doing." It sounded simple enough, or so I thought.

Following Mr. Brooks was an adventure. Due to his mental illness, he didn't focus too much on anything going on around him. However, at the same time he would often hop a bus and disappear into traffic before you could say Jack Robinson. I lost him in downtown Uvalde on two consecutive nights. Uvalde is not a large town and a man with Schizophrenia kept giving me the slip. It started to get embarrassing. On several other nights he remained at home. It wasn't until the following week that I was finally able to discover what he was doing on the nights he disappeared.

That evening I sat in the dark in my surveillance vehicle not too far from his house. He lived in a small single-story wood frame home next to the Uvalde County Fairplex off Highway 90. I was hunched down in the plush leather driver's seat listening to jazz. The faint glow from the digital clock read 9:17 PM when I suddenly spied a dark figure walking down the sidewalk. It was him. I turned the key and slowly inched the car forward following him at a respectful distance. He turned right and headed in the direction of downtown. He walked up two blocks and then over three more and entered a rundown convenience store. A few minutes later he reappeared clutching a new pack of cigarettes and a can of beer. I watched as Fitz walked over to the side of the mini-mart and sat next to the dumpster. He then proceeded to drink the beer and smoke.

After finishing his beer, Fitz continued on foot downtown. He took a right on S. Wood Street past Evett's Bar-B-Que and walked into Municipal Park. As he faded into the darkness of the park I pulled over and got out of my car. I could feel a cool breeze on the back of my neck. The wind rustled through the trees and I heard a dog bark. In the distance, someone laughed abruptly and then broke into a coughing spasm. I walked through the darkness and instinctively felt my Beretta 9mm snug in a holster inside my waistband. I continued walking in the same direction and could no longer hear voices. As I got closer I could see that Fitz had descended down a muddy embankment and was sitting with several other people on the banks of the Leona River. That's where I saw Fitz buy crack from one of the dark shapes huddled next to the river. He had joined several other local homeless people there next to the river. They were sitting there sharing cigarettes and drugs. I followed him again on a subsequent night to a local crack house where it was more of the same. That's how I solved the disappearance of Mr. Brooks.

Not all the cases involving runaways, missing persons or kidnappings have ended well. I had a case in Laredo, Texas where, just like young Cruz Guzman, the child was allegedly ferried across the U.S. border into Mexico by a female relative.

However, in this case the details were a bit murky. The Federal Bureau of Investigationlxxviii was also involved in that investigation.

On a warm August afternoon, I was on surveillance watching the home of one of the relatives of the missing child. I looked in my rear-view mirror and saw a silver Ford Crown Victoria pull in quietly behind me. The driver, a well-dressed white male with gray hair in his fifties, exited the vehicle and casually walked up to my car. He identified himself as FBI Special Agent Nolan and stated he was working the same case. I showed him my private investigator identification and then he crouched down next to my driver's side window and we compared notes. I had heard plenty of tales of egotistical and dictatorial FBI agents. I don't know if those stories are true, but if so, Special Agent Nolan was the exception.

He said the FBI had surreptitiously placed a covert surveillance camera on a utility pole and had it pointed down at the relative's home. They had been monitoring the people coming and going from the home, but so far it hadn't produced any useful information. We were both grasping at straws. As previously mentioned, despite what you see on television, much of investigative work is actually tedious and boring. Apparently, even for the FBI.

Later that same day an adult female departed the residence. We believed her to be involved, at least on the periphery, in the child abduction. Both myself and Special Agent Nolan pulled in behind her and initiated a moving surveillance. At some point during our surveillance she must have realized she was being followed because she floored the gas pedal and took off like a rocket. We did too, accelerating at speeds of up to one hundred miles per hour on Interstate Highway 35. I was in communication with Agent Nolan by cell phone. When I told him I didn't want to get a speeding ticket he said, "Relax, you're with me." On hearing that, I floored the gas pedal to keep up with both of them. In that moment, I felt like a G-man chasing my suspect. The woman eventually exited the highway onto a busy downtown Laredo street where we lost sight of her. She more than likely quietly slipped into Nuevo Laredo, Mexico on one of the many narrow side streets.

I followed up on several other leads for the next month and continued my surveillance efforts, but unfortunately, I was never able to determine the child's whereabouts. The FBI hit a brick wall as well. The client eventually ran out of resources and I moved onto other assignments. Most cases can be solved by a combination of time, money and hard work. But contrary to what you may have heard, even the best investigators have their disappointments and their failures.

About this time Mike Farmer heard through the grapevine that I had begun working for one of his former clients. Understandably, he was very upset about it. He assumed I had stolen the client from him and hasn't spoken to me since. But the reality is he hadn't done any work for the client since the previous year. They had a disagreement with him and were looking for a new company. Sometimes the truth can be hard to perceive, as in the case of the vanishing husband and wife.

Pablo and Evangeline Gonzalez were both injured working for a large discount retailer in Boise, Idaho. Eva, as she was called, was a cashier and Pablo worked in receiving. As husband and wife, they were injured on the same day. In fact, the circumstances surrounding their accidents, both slip and falls, were eerily similar. Pablo and Eva filed their claims at the same time, saw the same doctor and ended up having regular physical therapy appointments from the same clinic. That is, until they went missing. They stopped showing up for medical and physical therapy appointments and no longer returned the claims adjuster's telephone calls. After about a month of no contact, I was sent out to conduct surveillance and find out what was going on.

The Gonzalez's lived in an older neighborhood in Nampa, Idaho, not far from Lakeview Park. Their front yard was surrounded by a chain link fence and whoever had designed the landscaping had gone nuts. The front yard contained so many trees, shrubs and thick vegetation that the house was barely visible from the road. The chain link fence included a gate in front of their driveway. This required either Pablo or Eva to open and close the gate in order to pull their distinctive yellow Volkswagen Beetle in or out of the driveway. It presented a perfect opportunity to get video of either subject in action. I quickly parked between two houses on a nearby cross street and began my surveillance. I guzzled down a cold bottle of water, pulled my video camera close and waited for some activity.

I did not have a picture of the Gonzalez's. But, as it turned out, I really didn't need one. I had a physical description. They were both about five feet tall and each weighed approximately 300 pounds. Pablo was balding on the top but had a long grey pony tail that reached the middle of his back. They both walked with canes despite being in their early fifties.

After two days of absolutely no activity and no sign of their vehicle I was stumped. I hit the street and began to canvass the neighborhood. I spoke with several neighbors on the street but regardless of who I spoke with no one seemed to know where they had gone. I was finally able to locate a neighbor who recalled

Pablo talking about a trip, but he couldn't remember any other details. I had reached a dead end. Or so I thought.

As I drove out of Boise on interstate 84, I happened to look up and see the exit for the Boise airport. On a hunch, I quickly exited S. Vista Avenue and turned right. The Boise airport was not very big, so I decided to check the small long-term parking lot. It was there that the mystery only deepened. Tucked away in the back of the long-term parking lot on the very last row was a dusty, dirty, yellow Volkswagen Beetle belonging to Pablo and Eva Gonzalez. The Gonzalez's had evidently flown the friendly skies to some as yet unknown destination. Judging from the dirty condition of their car, they had apparently been gone for a while.

In the murky world of the private eye, things are not always as they seem. I remember looking in the windows of the vehicle for blood or signs of foul play. There was no reason to suspect any. It was just something that Thomas Magnum on *Magnum, P.I.* always seemed to notice.

I made a couple of discreet inquiries and learned that Pablo and Eva had flown to visit their daughter who was in the military at Lackland Air Force Base in San Antonio. They had both requested time off from their employer, but it was only partially approved. So, they took matters into their own hands and filed an exaggerated workers comp claim in order to use the paid time off to visit their daughter. When they eventually returned to Idaho I had gathered enough video of the Gonzalez's to question the legitimacy of their workers comp claims. Shortly after their return they decided to retire. When it came to Pablo and Evangeline Gonzalez, the only thing missing was their integrity iking with neighbors, as in the case of Pablo and Eva, is almost always Having connections and local informants are a must to be successful in the private investigation business. I have conducted surveillance on several of the military bases in San Antonio, as well as Hill Air Force Base in Layton, Utah, from time to time. I had a local connection at Lackland who would arrange a temporary base pass whenever I needed it. I once surveilled a person suspected of insurance fraud who worked as a civilian on the base. With the help of my connection I was able to follow him to and from work.

I had another case where the claimant was married to a soldier and living on post at Ft. Sam Houston in San Antonio. Getting into Ft. Sam was much easier. I simply drove to what was then called Brook Army Medical Center, Ft. Sam's hospital right off interstate highway 35. Once there, I received a temporary post pass that was good for a couple of days to visit a sick friend. I'd then leave and head down Binz-Engelman Road where I then entered a different gate. I then drove over to on-post housing near the national cemetery and set up surveillance on my subject.

As a private investigator, you're sometimes expected to stretch the truth and bend the rules to solve a case. But I never break them. Of course, not all my experiences have resulted in formal investigations. I once had a conversation with a woman who told me she was hiding from the Church of Scientology.

I had begun teaching several adult and community education classes for a couple of local school districts in the San Antonio area. I called my class *Private Investigation 101*. It offered students a brief introduction to the private eye industry. I went over how to become a private eye, myths surrounding the business and what it is we really do. One evening, after I had just finished teaching a class, several students hung around to ask questions. Out of the corner of my eye I noticed an older woman who had attended the class standing back somewhat as if she was hesitant to ask a question. After everyone left I gathered up my laptop and projector and the woman accompanied me as I walked out to the parking lot. That's when she began to convey to me her strange tale.

She said she was originally from Clearwater, Florida where she had been a member of the Church of Scientology. She claimed to have worked as a staff member on the third floor of the Super Power Building, Scientology's large Flag Building on South Fort Harrison Avenue. While there, despite being married, she became involved in an extramarital affair with one of the top Scientology officials at that location. She told me his name, but I hadn't heard of him. As often happens in these cases, she became pregnant. According to the woman, the man with whom she had had the affair encouraged her to keep quiet and have an abortion. She refused. She decided to admit the affair and the pregnancy to her husband who was also a Scientologist. But her lover was adamant. He said she had to have an abortion and keep the affair quiet, due to his position in the church. He then, in no uncertain terms, threatened her. She then claimed that he said she'd be killed if she did not do what he told her. She was so frightened by this that she fled Florida and was living under an assumed name in Texas. She had been named a Suppressive Person by the sect. She claimed that Scientologists were trying to kill her. I don't know if what she told me was true. Perhaps some of it was an exaggeration. What I do know is that as we stood there in the parking lot next to her car at 9:00 PM at night shivering in the cold, I knew she believed it.

CHAPTER 14

TRUTH IS THE FIRST CASUALTY OF LOVE

Falling in love is exciting. The butterflies and the anticipation one feels can be as potent as an illicit drug. If the feelings are mutual, sparks fly when you first meet. But like a falling star, some love affairs burn brightly, if only for a short time. Some lovers eventually seek companionship in the arms of a stranger, leaving you with the cold, harsh reality of your partner's betrayal. Over time, those initial feelings of love slowly turn to contempt. Until one day you wake up next to a stranger. Something Rhonda Goodman learned all too well.

Rhonda lived in the Dominion, an upscale gated community set among the gentle rolling hills of the Texas Hill Country on the far northwest side of San Antonio. The Dominion covers about 1,500 rolling acres and the average price of a home is close to a million dollars. Notable residents include Grammy award winning country western singer George Strait, Academy award winning actor Tommy Lee Jones, actor and professional wrestler "Stone Cold" Steve Austin, as well as several current and retired professional athletes from the San Antonio Spurs.

Rhonda was married to Chase Goodman, a local architect. They had one daughter in high school and a marriage which had derailed many years ago. Rhonda had her friends, and Chase his, but they rarely did anything together. She knew Chase was seeing other women but had let it slide. She planned on filing for divorce once their daughter had graduated high school. As time passed, she arrived

at the point where she was ready to prove her husband's infidelity for th
And I acquired it for her. In a big way.

Typically, in infidelity cases, there's no smoking gun. In other words, we're usually able to document a couple entering a hotel or kissing in a parked car. That's generally enough to prove an illicit relationship exists. But it's rare to actually film anyone having sex. After a week of trailing Chase with little to show for it, I followed him to an area behind a Lowe's Home Improvement store near the intersection of Loop 1604 and Blanco Road. Imagine my surprise when, shortly after he arrived, a woman drove up in a black Audi. Chase opened the door of his white Hummer and stood there as the woman approached. She was tall with long red hair swept back into a pony tail. Red Hair was wearing a blue half t-shirt that occasionally offered a view of her black sports bra. She also wore black yoga pants that came down to just below her knees. She had a derriere so tight you could've bounced a quarter off it and put your eye out. I found out later she was an instructor at a local Bikram Yoga class. Chase left his driver's side door open and was standing outside the vehicle leaning back on his car. He and Red Hair began embracing. I was at the eastern end of the building. I couldn't risk moving any closer without arousing their suspicion. I slowly zoomed my camera in and that's when I got an eyeful.

There's a tremendous amount of pressure in the investigation business to obtain results. Especially with domestic clients. They've all watched too much television and believe what we do is fairly simple. I am already selling an intangible. I remind clients they're paying for my time and effort, not for any perceived outcome. I can't guarantee a particular outcome. Clients are understandably unhappy when the results are less than definitive. However, that was not going to be a problem this time. As I watched the couple, Red Hair slowly slid down to her knees in front of Chase. She unbuckled his belt and you can imagine what happened next. Right there behind Lowe's. In the parking lot. Next to the dumpster. It was going to break my client's heart, but she wanted to know. She needed to know.

Sometimes a client's suspicions turn out to be unfounded, as in the case of Jason Rankin. He had focused so long on what he believed to be true that he eventually lost the ability to discern between what was true and what he thought was true. Jason, like so many others, had developed his own narrative.

I met Jason in the parking lot of In-n-Out Burger in Centerville, Utah. I had the cheeseburger. He had the anxiety. His wife Jenny planned to attend a girl's weekend at the Hyatt Regency near The Embarcadero in San Francisco with four other women. The girls had known each other in college at The University of Utah, where they were members of the Alpha Chi Omega sorority. Jason suspected that given the opportunity, Jenny might engage in a brief fling during the trip. He had a reason for his suspicions.

A year prior, he had returned home early from a business trip. As he drove into town he happened to glance over and see Jenny's car in the parking lot of a grocery store on Parrish Road. Assuming she was shopping and excited to see her, he steered his car over to where hers was parked. However, as he drove closer, he noticed a black Ford pickup truck parked next to his wife's car. Jenny was sitting in the truck on the passenger side. A man Jason did not recognize was seated next to her.

Jason was taken back and unsure of what to do. His mind raced through all the potential reasons this situation could be legitimate. But he was left with the obvious conclusion. His wife was having an affair. Jason watched and waited to see if the nature of the relationship would be revealed. When nothing of the sort happened, he drove up next to her car and parked. Jenny happened to glance over at Jason in his vehicle. When she did, she displayed a look of surprise on her face. A look that quickly turned to anger. She whispered something to the man in the truck and then exited his vehicle. As soon as she did, the stranger drove away, and Jenny walked over to Jason with a look of irritation on her face. The first thing out of her mouth was "Are you spying on me?" She explained that the stranger was someone she had known in college. She had happened to run into him and they were simply catching up on old times. Jason found this explanation dubious. But, with no evidence suggesting otherwise, he dropped the topic. But it had gnawed away at him ever since, like a grudge that quietly festered. Whenever Jenny did anything disagreeable, Jason would silently caress and nurture the grudge until it had consumed him. He would pay any amount of money to get to the truth. Jason would be at home taking care of their three-year-old daughter, Zoe, while Jenny cavorted with her college girlfriends in San Francisco. He had to be sure she would remain faithful on the trip.

If I was going to follow five women, I needed help. I reached out to Valerie, my wife and girl Friday; and a licensed private investigator in her own right. We took the red eye to San Francisco and stayed at a lovely cottage in San Rafael with a wonderful view of San Francisco Bay. The very next night we got down to business.

followed the ladies that weekend from their hotel to several restaurants around Fisherman's Wharf, including Coit Tower, Lombard Street and even Alcatraz. While they were having dinner one of those nights, Jenny and a couple of the other ladies suddenly excused themselves to use the restroom. Valerie immediately got up to follow them into the restroom in the hopes that Jenny would mention another man or her plans for the evening. But Valerie reported that nothing happened.

The restroom break turned out to be indicative of the whole trip. Nothing happened. Jenny remained on good behavior. There was some misbehavior going on, but it was committed by one of the other ladies. She had met up with a man at Hooters and he ended up going back to her hotel room. But Jason's wife remained faithful. Jason's suspicions were unfounded, at least during the weekend in question.

Sometimes a client's suspicions turn out to be true. But at other times it's all in their head. It's the not knowing that's the worst. Often the truth isn't known until the client hires a private investigator. There are two versions of the truth in every divorce; his and hers. In my experience, it's usually a bit of both, but mostly in between. Author Clare Boothe Luce once said, *"No good deed goes unpunished."* Something I learned very well from Humberto Paz.

Paz was a successful accountant with an office on Coalton Road near the Interlocken Golf Club in Broomfield, Colorado. Everything about Paz was average. He was average height with an average build and average looks. He hired me to conduct surveillance on his ex-wife Raquel during the weeks she had custody of their son James, whom they both affectionately referred to as "Pinto." They shared custody of the five-year-old who spent alternating weeks with either parent. Paz was angling for the upper hand in the custody arrangement. I met him at his office where I asked about his suspicions. The mild-mannered accountant didn't hold back. He suddenly became very agitated.

"She's a whore." He said. I thought that was a rather harsh way to describe the mother of his child. Little did I know he was just getting warmed up. "She's a crazy bitch. She's a damn thief and a liar. And she uses drugs. She lives with her sister and her mother. All the family uses drugs. She sleeps with a different man every night and hangs out with drug dealers."

Paz wanted me to gather evidence so that he could get Pinto out of that environment. On the face of it, I didn't blame him. I would do the same. However, with many domestic cases, what a client says and what the truth is, can be two entirely different things.

I continued questioning Paz to get more background information. What I got was an earful. It could've been a made-for-television movie. Paz may have been average in many ways, but he was also brilliant. He had spent the first part of his life focused solely on his education. His only date was an accounting text book. The only figure he was interested in was compound interest. He was somewhat of a social maladroit. He was educated in everything except what some women are capable of.

He eventually opened his accounting firm and it had made him very wealthy. And then he hired Raquel as a secretary. She was quite the opposite of Paz and anything but average. She had long, soft, auburn hair that cascaded gently to her shoulders and sky-blue eyes that anyone and everyone seemed to get lost in. To say she was beautiful was an understatement. He was wealthy and lonely. She was beautiful and poor. She had a stunning body. He had nobody. It was a lethal combination.

Paz told me that soon after he hired Raquel she began to flirt with him. He insisted he never had a chance. He said she wore pencil skirts and low-cut blouses that were always a little too tight revealing her breasts and highlighting her perfect figure. Her looks always lingered a little too long. Paz liked the way their hands accidently brushed against each other whenever she handed him paperwork. She was the kind of woman that could make a man forget his own name. Paz explained this to me in much the same way a fourteen-year-old boy would talk about his first crush. He was attracted to her but with no real experience with women, he had no idea what to do. Moreover, the thought never entered his mind that beginning a relationship with an employee could spell disaster.

Then one afternoon it just happened. He said they were the only two left in the office. Paz was seated at his desk going over paperwork when she walked in to show him some spreadsheets. Raquel walked over to the side of his desk to hand the documents to him when some of the paperwork accidently slipped out of the folder and fell under his chair. He turned to face her and, in an attempt to pick up the documents, they both bent forward together at the same time bumping heads. They looked at each other and had a good laugh about it but then suddenly their looks became serious. Paz felt his blood pressure rise and he was suddenly very thirsty. Raquel was on her knees facing him, her striking blue eyes looking up at him. Without warning, and in a highly uncharacteristically bold move for the shy accountant, Paz closed his eyes, grabbed her arms, pulled her body close to his and kissed her. And as fast as you can say accounts receivable, she moved into his Boulder, Colorado condominium on Foothills Parkway the next week.

Four weeks later Raquel was pregnant and a month after that they hopped a direct flight from Denver to Las Vegas where they were married in a little white wedding chapel on the Vegas strip. It happened that quickly.

As with most relationships however, the newness and the excitement eventually subsided. They reluctantly retreated to the boredom and the routine of daily life that all lovers experience. And then Raquel needed money for maternity clothes because her old ones no longer fit. She needed money for a manicure because a wealthy accountant's wife had to look good. She asked Paz for money to meet her friends for lunch at Jill's Restaurant in Boulder. Then she needed money to remodel his home, now their home, because they had a baby on the way, and really, how could anyone live like this? Then Raquel's unemployed mother, Rita moved in because, well…she had nowhere to go. And besides, she could help after the baby was born. Rita must have had a hole in her pocket because she was always borrowing money from Raquel. Money Raquel got from Paz. And money that Rita never seemed to pay back. Then Raquel's spending at Cherry Creek North Shopping Center in Denver became increasingly expensive. Paz told me Raquel got arrested for shoplifting. Twice. When he confronted Raquel about the shoplifting charges she became angry and quit her job. For Paz, a man accustomed to the fixed and precise processes of mathematics, his predictable, average life was spiraling out of control.

Although Paz was wealthy, his new wife was spending money like a drunken sailor. In an effort to control the hemorrhaging of his bank accounts, he placed

Raquel on a strict allowance. This did not go over well with her. Later, he noticed items from his house missing and she admitted to selling them to a pawn shop for cash. Rita seemed unable to find a job, nor did she appear to be looking for one. She spent most her time watching daytime television and burning through a couple of packs of Virginia Slim's each day. The situation soon became untenable for Paz.

Somewhere in the midst of all this turmoil, Pinto was born. A perfectly, healthy beautiful baby boy with a thick head of hair. Paz told me that for the briefest of moments, despite the changes associated with having a newborn, everything in his life returned to normal. Raquel was a doting mother. Rita actually did help care for the child. But the new-found happiness was to be short lived.

Paz continued with his narrative. He told me after Pinto's birth, Raquel's interest in sex abruptly decreased until it was virtually non-existent. Furthermore, she showed no interest in even embracing or kissing him. All her warmth and caring seemed to be solely reserved for Pinto. Paz said he felt like a stranger in his own home. He told me Raquel would parade around the house wearing nothing but a thick white terry cloth bathrobe that she frequently forgot to close. Or sit by the pool in the backyard wearing a tiny string bikini. She was always just out of reach; almost as if she was teasing him. Several months after Pinto's birth, Paz first heard the rumors. Employees and even some of his clients said they had seen Raquel around town with other men. She would often leave late at night and return early the next morning without offering a plausible explanation as to her whereabouts. This roller coaster nightmare would continue for another two years.

Paz said that when he attempted to talk to Raquel about these issues she became unhinged. According to him, she was already unstable and prone to fits of anger, conditions exacerbated by whatever drugs she was taking. The final straw occurred when she had the temerity to ask Paz to move out of his own house. That's when the shy accountant finally had an epiphany. He realized that something had to be done to put an end to this never-ending nightmare. And so, one afternoon he kicked her and Rita out of the house. He changed the locks and installed an alarm system and security cameras. He then hired a lawyer and filed for divorce. They ended up sharing custody of their son and Paz began paying child support each month. At least that was his side of the story.

He told me Raquel and Rita moved in with Raquel's younger sister Gloria and her husband Dwayne. They all lived together in an aging apartment complex off S. Lashley Lane on the south side of Boulder. He wanted to find something; anything that would give him an upper hand in their child custody arrangements. To be perfectly frank, he seemed more interested in that, than in Pinto's welfare. After Paz finished speaking he gave me Raquel's information and a check for my retainer. I left his office and went to work.

I conducted surveillance on Raquel for two solid weeks; a week when Pinto was staying with her and a week when he wasn't. However, what I found didn't coincide with what Paz had told me in his office that day. There must have been some truth to the shopping sprees because I never saw Raquel in the same outfit more than once during those two weeks. She was definitely a clothes horse. From her black patent leather Gucci platform pumps, to her Burberry cashmere trench coat this woman was always dressed to the nines. Of course, everything I knew about Raquel I had heard from Paz. Although I sensed much of it was exaggeration or speculation. Still, I could see why Paz fell hard for her. She was beautiful. She gave off sex appeal like gas fumes. One match and it would've all been over. But despite Paz's dreadful description of her behavior, I never observed any promiscuity. I never saw her with other men. I never observed her acting crazy or under the influence of drugs, other than enjoying a beer and a cigarette on the balcony of the apartment. She never stayed out late or engaged in risky behavior. I looked up her two shoplifting charges and discovered they were actually several years old; long before she had even met Paz. It was clear from the video I gathered that she loved Pinto and was completely devoted to him. In short, although I believe they had a stormy marriage and no doubt there were some major issues, it was in the past. Much of what Paz had told me was simply not true. After following her day and night for over two weeks, I found no evidence to suggest she was anything but a good and decent mother.

I wrapped up my report and presented it to Paz. I dropped it off at his office and a week went by without hearing anything. I finally telephoned him to see if he had any questions. When he answered the phone he verbally laid into me like a Pit bull on a Poodle. He went on and on about how Raquel had fooled me, that she was a whore, she was crazy, she was on drugs, etc. I tuned him out. I'd heard this record before. I tuned back in when he mentioned another private investigation firm. He admitted to hiring another PI firm before me and they had come to the same conclusion and provided the same results. Raquel had fooled them too, he said. She was a...well, you get the picture. He was one angry accountant.

It occurred to me that he had spent the last few years convincing himself that things were a certain way when they simply were no longer that way, if they ever had been. Clearly, much of the anger and craziness that Paz attributed to Raquel belonged solely to him.

I hung up the phone and sat and stared at it for a few minutes. Raymond Chandler said, *"There are two kinds of truth: the truth that lights the way and the truth that warms the heart."* The truth Paz believed in didn't fit into either category. He was a bitter, angry man. Considering his experience with Raquel I really couldn't blame him. But she had moved on. I poured myself an ice-cold Dr. Pepper and I moved on too.

In our criminal justice system when it comes to guilt or innocence there are always extenuating circumstances. They're not excuses but contributing factors as to why what happened really happened. They must be understood, so that the crime may be understood. Crime, like life, doesn't happen in a vacuum. When it comes to sentencing and convictions and justice in general, things are not always fair. Which brings me to the investigation of Karen "Bunny" Meyer, the pugilistic ex-wife.

Bunny was in her early 40's and although her beauty had faded somewhat it was clear she took care of herself. She had a body that would, according to Raymond Chandler's book *Farewell, My Lovely*, *"...make a Bishop kick a hole in a stained-glass window."*[lxxix]

Bunny married Jimmy when she was 17 and bore him six beautiful children. He then traded her in for a newer model. A trophy wife. A young, bleach-bottle blonde named Lacey Hopkins. What added insult to injury was the fact that Lacey was 24 years old. The same age as Jimmy and Bunny's oldest daughter.

Jimmy and Bunny were originally from Kensington, Maryland but Jimmy had moved the family to the small rural town of Morgan, Utah. It was there Jimmy had met Lacey in the drive-thru at the local McDonald's on South State Street. He wanted a Big Mac. Lacey wanted a Sugar Daddy. Later that week Jimmy began picking up Lacey after work and, despite the almost twenty years' difference in their ages, they began having a torrid affair. Morgan is a small town and folks began to take note of Jimmy's gold Chrysler Town and Country. It always seemed to be parked in random parking lots or out-of-the-way areas throughout the town late at night.

A month later Jimmy filed for divorce. He kicked Bunny out of the house and the very next day Lacey moved in. Unbelievably Jimmy, at least temporarily, retained custody of their children and the house.

A week passed, and Bunny stopped by one afternoon to retrieve some clothes she had left behind. Jimmy was at work and the children at school. Bunny knocked on the door of her former home and was greeted by an upbeat Lacey who let her in. Their conversation was civil, and everything was fine, until Bunny walked into the master bedroom. Throughout their twenty-five-year marriage, wherever they had resided, Bunny and Jimmy had always kept their wedding photograph in a special silver frame on the headboard of their bed. Upon entering the bedroom, Bunny looked over at the bed and there, placed carefully in the center of the shelf on the headboard was a wedding photo in the silver frame. However, it had been replaced with the wedding photo of Jimmy and his new wife, Lacey.

According to Lacey, Bunny lost it. She became hysterical. She began to pummel Lacey who was eventually able to run to the front door and somehow push Bunny out of the house. When Jimmy returned from work later that day he found Lacey with a black eye and a split lip. He immediately called the police. Statements were taken. And although she denied it, Bunny was arrested for assault and battery.

But just like the case of Paz and Raquel, things are not always as they seem. During my investigation for Bunny I found a neighbor who had been working in his garage nearby. He happened to see Lacey and Bunny exit the residence the day of Bunny's visit. According to the neighbor, Lacey looked fine. No black eye. No split lip. The ladies even sat on the front steps and talked for a while, before hugging and waving goodbye. If that was the case, then something wasn't right. Upon further questioning I discovered that Jimmy had become enraged after learning that Bunny had stopped by while he was at work. Desperate to rid himself of Bunny once and for all, he hatched a plan. It was Jimmy that administered the black eye and busted lip to Lacey. His new wife willingly submitted to Jimmy's beatings because she didn't want him to leave her.

The lesson here is to never make assumptions in an investigation. Leave no stone unturned in your pursuit of the truth. There may be different perspectives by those involved but there's only one truth. It's an investigator's job to sift through the innuendo and emotions and discover the indisputable facts. That's what I did and that's how I learned that Jimmy and Lacey had lied. And that's how I was able to spring Bunny from jail.

After this investigation, I was home relaxing one afternoon when something very bizarre happened. My infant son Dylan was asleep in an adjacent bedroom with a baby monitor attached to his crib. I had the receiver end of the baby monitor on a lamp table as I watched television. Suddenly, static came from the receiver and I heard a man's voice very distinctively say "Hey baby, how are you?" The hairs on the back of my neck stood on end. I think I did the standing broad jump from the living room to my son's bedroom expecting to confront a would-be kidnapper. But my son was sound asleep in his crib. No one else was in the room. Nevertheless, the man's voice continued coming from the receiver. It appeared to be a one-sided telephone conversation that I had somehow picked up on the baby monitor. I lived in an apartment complex and apparently, someone was using a cordless telephone nearby. I discovered later on that baby monitors and the very first cordless telephones operated on the same radio frequencies. It was clear from the telephone call that the man, whomever he was, was married. Apparently, he was having an affair with the woman on the other line, although I could not hear her side of the conversation. At one point, he said "Baby, she's almost here. I'm gonna go check." Like a good detective, I quickly ran to the front window of my apartment and slowly parted the blinds. I peered out at the complex when I saw him. Directly across from my unit my neighbor had opened his door and was looking around. He had a cordless telephone to his left ear. He continued speaking and now I could both see and hear the conversation. Eventually he hung up and I watched as his wife and two young sons returned home. I turned around slowly and slid back down on my couch. I had known they were having marital difficulties and now I understood why. It came as no surprise when they eventually divorced. This was exemplary of the types of cases I would deal with throughout my career. But it's always painful when it's someone you know personally.

CHAPTER 15

DO ALL STRIPPERS DRIVE CADILLAC ESCALADES?

Talk to just about any private investigator long enough and the conversation will eventually come around to cases that involved strippers. I don't know why that is. But, for some reason in each investigation the strippers all look the same. Five-four, one hundred and twenty-five pounds with a recent breast augmentation. And they all drive Cadillac Escalades. My next case would involve a foul-mouthed ex-stripper, links to organized crime, a fake workers compensation clinic and an informant named Mr. Deacon. Mark Twain was right. Truth really is stranger than fiction.

Mr. Deacon was an African-American gentleman in his late sixties that worked as a security officer for a large self-insured public utility in Dallas. As is the case with many security officers he felt unappreciated. Largely ignored by his co-workers, he moved silently on tired feet throughout the facility checking door knobs and turning off lights. Though he was old, Mr. Deacon had excellent hearing. And like Frank Wills, the security guard who stumbled upon a break-in at the Watergate office complex in 1972, Mr. Deacon stumbled upon some juicy information.

He advised the public utility's claims adjusters that most the employees currently on workers' compensation, about nineteen in all, were being steered to the same chiropractic clinic on Mockingbird Lane. The clinic, as they say in Texas, was all hat and no cattle. In other words, it was a fake clinic without a chiropractor. It wasn't providing any real medical services. Claimants would show up for their appointments and file paperwork but receive no medical services in return. The clinic then sent a fake bill to the adjusters. Once the bill was paid the clinic would then kickback a small percentage to the employee for their trouble.

Unfortunately, this type of insurance scam is more common than you think. Because of this I have conducted numerous random clinic inspections for insurance companies. The inspections are carried out to confirm the clinic has the proper equipment to treat patients, as well as credentialed medical personnel on site.

During my investigation of this location, I learned that the clinic was allegedly owned by a man in Houston with ties to organized crime. His girlfriend, Crystal Thomas, managed the facility. She had shoulder length bleach blond hair and was a former stripper that had gone by the stage name of Layla. It was Mr. Deacon who found out that Layla had called a meeting of all the workers comp claimants for the following week. This meeting would present an excellent opportunity for me to identify everyone involved.

Prior to that meeting, I got together with the public utility's claims adjusters to go over our game plan. Rather than run the risk of being seen by any of the claimants at the adjuster's offices, we met at Rudy's, a local bar-b-que restaurant. This was done out of an abundance of caution.

As we sat and enjoyed mouth-watering bar-b-que on red and white checkered tablecloths, Frieda, the head adjuster, carefully explained the details of the investigation. She wanted video of all the employees coming and going to the meeting with close-ups of their faces. Once they were all identified at this meeting we would then focus a separate workers' compensation surveillance on each of them. I was assisted by three other investigators, Stu Hall, Julio Escobar and Lloyd Barnes.

On a cool Fall afternoon, Stu, Julio, Lloyd and I headed to the medical building where Crystal had her clinic. The clinic was on the first floor of a three-story office building with parking in an underground parking lot. We took up different positions throughout the parking lot affording each of us a different vantage point. Collectively, we would be able obtain close-ups of the claimant's faces and identify the license plate of the vehicle in which they arrived. We would be able to confirm which of the claimants were visiting Crystal's clinic.

I obtained video of Crystal as she arrived in her blue Cadillac Escalade. She exited the vehicle wearing a pink Mohair sweater dress and black boots that came up to just below her knees. Her skin was clear and as fine as porcelain. But, to quote Raymond Chandler, she "...*looked about as inconspicuous as a tarantula on a slice of angel food.*"lxxx She seemed to have a permanent scowl that otherwise would have been a beautiful face. She grabbed her Michael Kors designer handbag and made her way towards the building entrance.

Due to the limited parking, the office building employed a garage attendant to make sure reserved spaces stayed available and that only people with business in the building parked in the lot. Unfortunately, he seemed to take notice of both me and Julio's vehicle's immediately. I'm not sure why. I suspect it was because we arrived and parked but never exited our cars. We didn't know it at the time, but this garage attendant would prove to be our undoing. We had already obtained video of about twelve of the company employees when the proverbial poop hit the fan.

As she made her way to the building entrance, Crystal walked by the attendant's small parking station. That's when he motioned to her, indicating he needed to speak with her. She walked over and stepped inside the booth out of my view. It would not be until after the entire incident that I was able to view the video footage Lloyd had obtained. His video, shot from a different angle, showed the attendant talking to Crystal and pointing in the direction of me and Julio.

Some men will do just about anything to curry favor with a beautiful woman, especially one that looked like Crystal. The garage attendant was no different. It became clear that she had advised him to be on guard for anything out of the ordinary, a necessary precaution when you're running a phony chiropractor clinic. He evidently advised her of our surveillance, although they had no idea who we were or why we were there. She just knew there was something wrong. And that's when Crystal lost it. All five feet, four inches and one hundred and twenty-five pounds of this ex-stripper went absolutely ballistic.

She literally ran back to her Escalade and jumped in. The wheels squealed, and I could hear the transmission gears grind as she slammed it into reverse. Crystal then peeled around the parking garage until she came to a screeching halt behind my van. She had effectively blocked me in. Crystal then jumped out and began banging on my car windows and yelling. She dropped F-bombs and suggested I do things to myself that were physically impossible. Due to the tint and my surveillance curtains she couldn't observe who, if anyone, was inside the vehicle. She then ran over to Julio's vehicle and gave an encore performance. Julio was amused and turned the camera on her as she gave him the one finger salute, although with the limousine tint on his vehicle she couldn't see him either. Things were getting out of hand.

She commanded the parking attendant to call the police and he dutifully complied. As soon as I heard her say that, I also called the police. I told them a woman had blocked me from exiting my parking space and was totally out of control. I called the police too because I needed to throw suspicion away from the investigation. I also called Lloyd on my cell phone and told him to quietly depart the area as soon as he could do so without raising suspicion. I called Julio and told him to do the same thing as soon as Crystal's attention was diverted. My vehicle was blocked in. I wasn't going anywhere. I didn't have time to call Stu. Although the surveillance was blown I knew she had no real idea as to who we were or why we were there. It was time to protect our client, cut our losses and come back another day.

The police showed up and I got out of my van to offer my side of the story to the officer. All the while Crystal continued in rare form. She persisted in screaming and yelling obscenities at the top of her lungs as her voice echoed throughout the underground garage. I've never heard language like that before from anyone. And I was in the Army. In the infantry. In a war. Even the female police officer couldn't seem to calm her down. I decided that taking the exact opposite posture would boost my credibility with the police. And it worked. While all this was going on both Julio and Lloyd quietly pulled out of the parking lot and disappeared. Stu stayed ensconced in his surveillance position and was able to document a few other company employees.

In the end, despite being burned, we were able to document all of the public utility's claimants and their vehicles. The female police officer eventually escorted Crystal out of earshot. I told the police officer that I was the one that had called the police. I said I was a private investigator working a domestic case and had followed my subject into the garage. I had no idea who that woman was or why she had focused her attention on me. The officer listened to me and then casually glanced over at Crystal who was gesticulating wildly saying "They're everywhere! There's one in that green car!" Of course, Julio's green sedan was now nowhere in sight. The police officer then slowly turned back to me with a rather annoyed look on his face. "That woman's nuts." He said. "You can go ahead and get out of here."

I backed my vehicle up and drove away. The last thing I saw in my rear-view mirror was Crystal yelling at the police. Her pink Mohair sweater dress was swaying back and forth like clothes on the line being buffeted by a gentle summer breeze. But there was nothing gentle about Crystal.

I was once hired by a woman in Columbia, Missouri who suspected her husband was visiting a strip club and cheating on her with one of the strippers. Lois and Larry Carr had been married for twenty years. As she explained, their marriage had slowly become more of a friendship without romance. They had a good relationship, but Larry no longer showed any interest in sex and hadn't for quite some time. In fact, the last time they had been intimate was six months prior and that was because it was Lois' birthday. Lois was convinced there was someone else. She knew Larry frequented the Kitty Kat Lounge on Vandiver Drive and ultimately feared he would leave her. Lois wanted to know what was going on.

I began to follow Larry after work and on weekends, however he didn't do much of anything. He always drove just under the speed limit and came to a full and complete stop at all stop signs. Everything Larry did was slow and methodical. He had my vote for the world's most boring human. All Larry seemed to do was drive to work, get gas and go home. Occasionally he would stop at the grocery store on his way home.

After several days of this I began to think that perhaps I should tell Lois her fears were unfounded. Larry hadn't stepped foot in the Kitty Kat Lounge or any other strip club. Everything he did was routine and predictable. Until one Friday afternoon when he left work early and headed, not in the direction of home, but west on Interstate 70 in the direction of Kansas City. Maybe this was going to get interesting after all.

About a half hour later he abruptly took the exit for the city of Boonville, and then turned onto highway 40. Larry's beige Ford Taurus eventually came to a stop at a small white windowless building surrounded by a high chain link fence. He drove into the parking lot, exited the car and then casually walked in the front door.

There was a small sign over the business that said "Gym." But something about the place seemed off. It was on the outskirts of the City of Boonville and lacked the hustle and bustle normally associated with a gym. Furthermore, Larry was dressed in business casual clothes and hadn't carried a gym bag into the establishment. There were several other cars scattered throughout the parking lot. The place was in a state of disrepair and was giving me a slightly off kilter reading. I continued to see middle aged men come and go.

I eventually made some inquiries and that's when I discovered that it was a gym. At least not in the traditional sense. I discovered it was spa that catered exclusively to gay men. That probably explained Larry's singular disinterest in sex; at least with Lois. For the briefest of moments, I considered going in and obtaining covert video of him in flagrante delicto. But the thought left my mind as soon as it entered. I've always been a live and let live kind of guy. And despite my profession I've never been judgmental of what people do in their personal time but going in there undercover as a gay man was something I just couldn't fake. Besides, I had a much more difficult task ahead of me. I had to go back and explain to Lois what I had learned. I did so in a delicate and sensitive manner. She didn't react with much surprise when I disclosed the results of the investigation. Perhaps she had long suspected Larry of batting for the other team. But it was a hard thing for a wife of twenty years to hear.

As a private investigator, I am not always able to help people the way I would like. The case of Lois and Larry Carr was a good example. My findings didn't really provide Lois any peace of mind. It only left her with more questions. Sometimes it's because I just can't solve the case. Other times it's because the client ultimately decided not to take my recommendations or to even hire me. Like Donna.

She called me from Las Vegas one evening where she worked at a strip club on Paradise Road. It was there Donna had met a certain former professional athlete. They became involved in a torrid romance that eventually grew violent. She had broken off the relationship, but he often telephoned her and threatened her. Lately, she had the uneasy feeling that someone had been in her apartment.

Several of her personal items seemed to be out of place, as if someone had moved them. I gave her some free advice and then outlined several other things I could do to help her. Donna said she'd think about it and give me a call me back. I never heard from her again and I soon forgot about the call.

It's not uncommon to receive random telephone inquiries concerning potential investigations, and then never hear from the prospective client again. In fact, it's quite normal in this business. Sometimes the potential client is unprepared to pay for an investigation and at other times they're just not ready to pull the trigger. Fast forward almost three years later and I was looking through the news when a story caught my eye. It was about a former professional athlete who had killed his ex-girlfriend in a fit of anger. It turned out to be the very same Donna who had called me for help so long ago. I can't say that I wasn't surprised. But I wish I could've been there for her.

I was there for another woman. But only because she was committing personal injury fraud. She had been involved in a serious auto accident on Interstate 80 near Park City, Utah. Her name was Bailey Christensen and she was clipped by a semi-trailer truck as she drove through Parley's Canyon on the way to Salt Lake City. Although she was legitimately injured, there was some question as to the extent and permanency of her injuries. According to Bailey's attorney they were severe, life threatening and permanent. She'd be lucky to ever work again. Because of the nature of her injuries Bailey's attorney was asking for a one-million-dollar settlement.

With such a high dollar claim the insurance company faced a tremendous exposure. They would need a private investigation company to look into it. They ordered an activity check; a quick, simple surveillance to determine th Bailey's injuries and her level of daily activity. Based on the results of check more surveillance might be warranted. Initially, I had some difficulty trying to locate her. She had moved recently without leaving a forwarding address. It would be some time before her new address would appear in my proprietary databases. So, I hit the streets and began knocking on doors; utilizing some old-fashioned shoe leather in an effort to locate Bailey.

I began where a private investigator always begins. With Bailey's last known address from four weeks before. From there, I would knock on doors, ask questions and attempt to cut that four-week time line down. Her last known address was a beautiful apartment complex in a secluded, wooded area of Holladay, Utah. I knocked on the doors of her closest neighbors but was unable to find anyone home. As a last resort, I walked over to the apartment office.

At the office I spoke with McKenna, the leasing manager, who was instantly bubbly and nauseatingly friendly until she discovered why I was there. She then promptly changed her attitude and wouldn't provide many details. As a general rule, the nicer the apartment complex, the less willing they are to provide information. The converse is also true. But it's no crime to ask questions. Sometimes you can continue asking questions in the hopes that the subject will begin to provide at least some information. McKenna stated again that she simply could not provide any information about Ms. Christensen's forwarding address. But she then said, "Why don't you just try to reach her at the club?"

"The club?" I wasn't sure what she was talking about. The rotary club? The Kiwanis? The health club?

"The strip club," she replied. Suddenly, what had begun as a simple activity check was getting interesting. McKenna continued, "I think she's a stripper at that club in Salt Lake. But, you already knew that, right?"

I didn't know anything about it. But I employed a common tactic used by investigators. I pretended to already be in possession of the facts. "Yeah, I knew she was a dancer." I said. "She works at that club over on…uh…" I feigned a sudden loss of memory over the exact details. As if on cue, McKenna finished my sentence offering up the needed information.

"…on 700 West. I forget the name," she said. Works every time. I thanked McKenna and took off for the strip club.

As it turned out it would've been easier to get information from the CIA. The strip club in question was called The Pink Lady and they were very protective of their employee's privacy as all strip clubs are. All manner of questionable people frequent these types of clubs. As a result, the ladies use pseudonyms and the clubs protect their identity to safeguard them from becoming victims of stalkers or other deranged fans.

It was late in the afternoon and the place had just opened. Vendors were wheeling cases of beer into a storage room near the bar and a fellow that looked like a sumo wrestler was pulling wooden chairs off the tops of tables. A variety of multi-colored flashing lights surrounded the stage. But with no dancers performing yet and no customers in the establishment, it looked like a sad circus. I ended up speaking with Vince, one of the managers. He was a tall, gangly fellow wearing a silk disco shirt, circa 1973. The kind with wide lapels. He also sported a silver arrowhead necklace and kept picking his teeth throughout our conversation. I wanted to tell him the 1970's called, and they want their shirt back. But think it would be helpful in my situation. As it turns out, nothing would have helped. Vince was adamant. He wouldn't provide any of the ladies' names or addresses. I showed him a photograph of Bailey from an old Facebook page, but he wouldn't even look at it. He wouldn't identify any of the ladies by their stripper names either. He wouldn't even confirm whether or not Bailey worked there, as McKenna had suggested. Vince was absolutely no help. Frustrated, I went back outside, sat in my surveillance vehicle and put on my thinking cap. Obviously, this case was going to call for some creative, stroke of genius.

I conducted regular surveillance at The Pink Lady in the hope of finding Bailey's vehicle but never did. However, I did find Teddy. He was a short, overweight balding gentleman who appeared like clockwork every day at about 5:15 p.m. for happy hour. Teddy always wore the same loose blue tie and rumpled brown suit that looked as if it had been slept in. Probably because it had. But despite his disheveled appearance, Teddy was affable and open to my questioning. After ordering him a drink I told him I was a private eye working a probate case and Bailey had a big inheritance check coming to her; if I could find her. He didn't know anyone at the club named Bailey. I showed my new friend the photograph of Bailey. He looked at it for a moment and after spitting ice cubes back into a glass said, "that looks a lot like one of the girls on the A crew. But they don't come in until about eight o'clock or so."

Before I had a chance to asked him any further details he continued. "They always have their hair and makeup all done up, so I don't know if it's the same girl. But the girl I'm thinking of only works weekends." Teddy knew his stuff. He said her nom de guerre was Tiny Bell. Clearly, Teddy had no life outside his almost daily trips to the Pink Lady. Armed with this new information I left Teddy sitting on his barstool.

I made it back to the Pink Lady the following Friday at two in the morning. I had barely pulled in and turned the engine off when Bailey Christensen, a.k.a. Tiny Bell, exited a door on the side of the club. I recognized her right away from her photo. She casually walked out of the parking lot and across the street to a multi-level parking garage. No wonder when I checked the license plates of the vehicles at the Pink Lady I had no success. Tiny Bell jumped into a shiny white Cadillac Escalade, turned on the engine and took off; her tires squealing through the parking garage.

She eventually exited Interstate 15 onto Interstate 80 and I followed her up through Parley's Canyon being careful to keep a respectful distance behind her. After about forty minutes she led me to her new condominium in Park City on Jupiter View Drive. Evidently the stripping gig was paying well. She pulled into a garage and then the door closed automatically.

Over the course of the next several days I conducted surveillance on Tiny Bell. Other than working at the Pink Lady on the weekends she wasn't very active. The assumption was made that, given the fact that she was a stripper, she had recovered from the injuries she sustained in the accident. The only recourse was to conduct covert surveillance inside the strip club. I happened to be out of town involved in another complex investigation at the time, so I turned the surveillance of Tiny Bell over to my associate, Chris Young. However, I did view the video evidence later.

Insurance claims surveillance is conducted to determine whether or not a subject's physical activities are within the scope of their alleged injuries. This, coupled with a medical evaluation, can provide evidence as to whether the injuries are permanent and debilitating. Tiny Bell had filed a personal injury claim after the accident. My job was to obtain video of Tiny Bell to allow the adjusters and medical personnel to come to a fair assessment.

Chris entered the Pink Lady that Saturday night, covert camera in hand, prepared to obtain video of Tiny Bell in action. The irony is that, given that strippers wear very little clothing, you would think that she would've been easy to identify inside the club. That was not the case. Teddy was right. Her hair and makeup were so over the top that Chris later told me if they hadn't announced her stripper name when she came out he wouldn't have recognized her. Needless to say, Bailey's performance as Tiny Bell was a crowd pleaser. And Teddy had a table up front. My client would be happy as well. To suggest that Tiny Bell was in good shape would be an understatement. In fact, she was performing physical activities that were not only well outside the parameters of her purported injuries, they were also well beyond what most normal people are capable of, other than perhaps the U.S. Women's Olympic gymnastics team. And no, that is not hyperbole.

Despite our evidence the case ended up going to trial. However, the judge deemed our undercover video "too obscene" to show a Utah jury. But not before he requested a personal copy of the video himself for "further legal evaluation," whatever that meant. I was disappointed in the judge's decision. The fact that Tiny Bell was a stripper meant nothing to me. She could've just as easily been a roofer or construction work. The evidence clearly showed that she was nowhere near as incapacitated as her attorney claimed. But, what can you do? As it turned out the lawyers ended up settling. Tiny Bell had initially been legitimately injured in the accident, so she did receive a couple hundred thousand dollars for medical bills and pain and suffering. But because we could show that she was in no way permanently incapacitated, her monetary award was well below the million dollars her attorneys had hoped for. I saved the client eight hundred thousand dollars. They considered it a win. I was unable to be there with Chris to get the goods on Tiny Bell because I had flown back to Houston for yet another theft investigation at Caliente Sabroso Foods. My prediction from so many years ago had finally come true.

CHAPTER 16

THIEVES, FRAUDS AND SCAMS

In Arthur Conan Doyle's book, *Sign of the Four*, Sherlock Holmes uttered his famous dictum, *"...when you have eliminated the impossible, whatever remains, however improbable, must be the truth."* This was something I would see again and again in my investigations. Like the Case of the Missing Tortillas, Part II.

Rocky Sepulveda, the senior facility manager at Caliente Sabroso Foods, had contacted me again. He said they had yet another theft problem on their hands and wanted to know how quickly I could be there. I wasn't surprised. I had been expecting his call.

Years earlier, when Mario and I had helped nab the two thieves responsible for the first theft, I had given Rocky a warning. Unless the company upgraded their security equipment and made some operational changes, the same thing was bound to happen again. Like the round shape of a tortilla, life has a funny way of coming full circle. Fast forward four years and I was meeting Rocky again about another theft problem.

I flew out the very next day landing at William P. Hobby Airport on the southeast side of Houston. I then rented a car for the short drive to Caliente Sabroso and was in Rocky's office by early afternoon. He confirmed they were coming up short on their inventory again. This time he suspected it was the closing crew at the warehouse. But he needed proof.

Things had changed very little since my first visit to Caliente Sabroso, although they had moved to a larger warehouse in the same general area. The closing crew worked until about midnight each night. The warehouse was at the lonely end of commercial complex near the highway. It faced another warehouse in the same business park. The two warehouses were about seventy-five yards apart with employee parking spaces and a few tractor trailers in between. Unlike the last time, there was no suitable vantage point to conduct surveillance.

Since I was back in Texas and would need assistance on this case, I contacted Stu Hall, my former co-worker at Mike Farmer Investigations, and we got down to business. Logistically, we had a problem. The closing crew were keenly aware of all the vehicles that belonged in the parking lot between the two warehouses. They would obviously be alerted to any vehicle with which they were unfamiliar. As an alternative, we had Rocky rent a mini-van and park it in front of the opposite warehouse where it remained for about week. He told the closing crew the van had been used by a salesman and it would be picked up in a few days. Each night, I would sneak into the van under the shroud of darkness and observe the closing crew through the open warehouse garage doors for any evidence of pilferage. It turned out to be a comedy of errors.

The first night I opened the car door without disengaging the alarm. In doing so, the alarm was set off for twenty seconds while I tried to figure out how to stop it. I ended up having to abandon my surveillance attempt for that night. The next night when I got in the vehicle all the interior lights came on when I opened the driver's door. In an attempt to get in and get the lights off I ended up hitting the horn with my rear end and announcing my presence loudly. Clearly, this was not

going well. Either way, it didn't seem to matter. The warehouse ⟨
attempt to steal company product during that time. It was finally Stu
with a clever solution.

He would scale the roof of the adjoining warehouse and shoot video of the malfeasance from above. I would remain nearby in my surveillance vehicle prepared to follow the employees to where they were stashing their ill-gotten booty. Although the crew would be alert to any surveillance attempt in the parking area, they would never think to look up on the roof of the adjacent warehouse. It would be Stu's idea that would break the case wide open. It was a brilliant and simple plan that, for the next week, still didn't provide any results. I began to wonder if maybe Rocky was wrong about the closing crew. But then one night it happened. The thieves struck with daring bravado. And little did I know it was to be a family affair.

About a week after my car alarm and horn fiasco, Stu and I showed up at the warehouse at about 10:00 pm. It was an unusually cold clear fall night with a biting wind blowing in from the North. We parked our cars at a commercial bakery across the street from the business park and quietly made our way on foot to the back of the bordering warehouse. Stu had brought a yellow tow rope with a hook on the end which, after several attempts, we were able to hook on to the last rung of a ladder that descended from the roof of the warehouse. For safety reasons, the ladder ended about 7 feet from the ground. Stu then began to pull himself up the rope towards the ladder like Batman. I gave him a boost, pushing him up until he was finally able to grasp the last rung of the ladder with his right hand. He quickly scaled the ladder all the way to the top. I watched below in the darkness as he

.lung his body on to the roof disappearing from sight. I then ran back to my car, jumped in and turned on the heater to warm up. My cell phone was on and everything appeared to be in order. I exhaled deeply and sat back and waited for his call.

From his solitary perch on the roof, Stu had a commanding view of Caliente Sabroso's warehouse below. He could see down into the large commercial garage doors. He sat there for about two hours shivering in the cold before anything happened. We stayed in constant contact by cell phone. Right about the time he said he could no longer feel his face due to the cold wind, it happened. One minute, the parking lot was quiet and still; the next minute it was like a scene from the movie, *The Italian Job* where the Mini Coopers all line up to have the gold bars loaded. As if on a pre-determined schedule, multiple vehicles began to arrive. Several pickup trucks and mini-vans drove up in front of Caliente Sabroso's warehouse where they parked side by side, all facing the same direction. Shortly thereafter, women and children emerged from these vehicles and walked into the warehouse. Stu raised his video camera and started recording. A few minutes later the closing crew, along with their wives and children, emerged from the warehouse carrying multiple boxes and bags of Caliente Sabroso's Mexican Food products. They began loading their personal vehicles and then returned inside for more. Bags and boxes of tortillas, picante sauce, taco shells and tortilla chips. You name it, they loaded it in their vehicles. The children laughed and giggled as they too carried stolen product, running alongside their thieving parents as if it was all fun and games. Each family made so many trips Stu began to lose count. The vehicles were filled to the brim. We later estimated that about $4,000.00 to $5,000.00 of product was stolen that night and learned that they had been doing it about twice a month for the last several months.

As they all began to depart, Stu notified me by cell phone and I pulled in behind one of the vehicles. I followed a family back to their apartment complex where I obtained video of them unloading their stolen plunder. On a subsequent night, I followed a different family home and watched as they backed their truck up to their garage. My jaw dropped when they opened the garage door. It was completely full of stolen Mexican food products. It was packed from floor to ceiling and from left to right. You couldn't get a butter knife in between the boxes.

In the end, the same scenario played out as it had the last time. Caliente Sabroso called the police and the employees were busted. And just like the last time they discovered after the fact that the supervisor of the closing crew had a criminal history. Evidently, he had been fired from his previous employer for stealing. Just like my earlier warning, I recommended to Rocky that the company make changes such as conducting pre-employment background investigations and upgrading their security cameras. Again, he demurred, stating that corporate was simply not willing to invest that kind of money. Pay me now or pay me later, I thought to myself. Caliente Sabroso Foods wouldn't invest in better security cameras. But Fred Hansen did. It was a bizarre investigation I call the Case of the Invisible Thief.

Fred was a spry eighty-five-year-old that lived alone on top of a mountain near Montrose, Colorado. Tall and thin with billowy white hair and a mischievous smile, he looked like everyone's favorite grandfather. As I drove to his house I carefully negotiated a long, gravel road and found myself winding my way up top of the mountain. New fallen snow had blanketed the pine trees the road somewhat treacherous. I looked out my car window at the drop off at the edge of the road and realized if my car slid off the road and down the cliff my body probably wouldn't be found until spring. As I crested the summit I recognized Fred's house sitting on about an acre of land clustered near a few other homes.

There is something peaceful about snow. Individual snowflakes seem so delicate and insignificant. They fall to the ground without a sound. Yet, I could hear the familiar crunch of the snow under my feet as I exited my car and walked over to Fred's front door. He opened the door as I climbed the last two steps to his front porch. He bent forward slightly as he walked but he was alert and engaging. I found him to be warm and friendly and he graciously invited me into his home. We sat at his kitchen table where he began to tell me about his recent burglary. I had been sent by the insurance company to interview Fred because his theft claim had raised several red flags. The adjuster believed his theft claim was fraudulent. Looking at the elderly man in front of me I found it hard to believe. But in this business anything is possible.

Fred presented me with a list of everything that had been stolen. It was a carefully prepared hand-written itemized list in a slightly sloping script. He had listed each item along with the value, the date it was purchased and even the serial numbers. The receipts for most of the items were also attached. He was sharp as a tack as he launched into the history and the use behind every purchase. Although he ultimately digressed and began talking about the science of Geology. I steered him back on track about the burglary. He answered my questions thoroughly and was most helpful.

As I interviewed him I slowly began to suspect that perhaps there was more going on than just a simple burglary. Despite the list and his total devotion to his burglary story, his home bore no obvious signs of forced entry. I inspected his doors and windows and discovered that he alone held the keys. He had no recent visitors. Fred seemed to think the perpetrators had gained entry through an unlocked window, but then he quickly admitted to always locking his doors and windows. He had gone so far as to install several expensive security cameras that monitored every door and every window on the exterior of his home.

He led me into his den where the security camera monitoring system was located. I immediately noticed a .45 caliber handgun lying on a small lamp table next to a recliner. For a fleeting moment, I considered where I was. A stranger's home on the top of a mountain in a rural area of western Colorado. I imagined for a second that Fred was a serial killer and filed fraudulent insurance claims so he could capture and kill claims adjusters and private investigators. I snapped out of my day dream when Fred began talking about his security system. I was carrying my concealed 9mm Beretta handgun, so I wasn't too worried about Fred.

I used the DVR on Fred's system to bring up video from the day the theft had occurred. He stated the theft had to have happened between noon and three in the afternoon when he was in town running errands. However, when I navigated the digital file to that exact time window, the video was absolutely blank. It was as if it had deliberately been erased. Apparently, someone had turned off the cameras for three hours that afternoon. Fred attributed it to the sneaky thieves.

Then he said something that piqued my curiosity. He said the local sheriff came out to investigate the burglary but refused to file a police report. I found that very odd. Especially with Fred's carefully itemized list of everything that was missing.

Throughout our almost one-hour conversation Fred had frequently uttered the phrase "they all think I'm crazy." I didn't pay much attention to it at first, assuming he was just waxing hyperbolically. He was referring to his neighbors, the sheriff and his adult daughter that lived nearby. I presumed it was his way of saying that no one was taking him seriously. But the more he said it, the more I considered it. Faced with the odd facts surrounding Fred's burglary, I began to consider an alternative explanation.

It wasn't until I spoke with Fred's next-door neighbor Phyllis and Fred's daughter Andrea, that I was able to confirm my suspicions about what had really happened. Or, had not happened, as the case may be. I went over the facts again in my mind. No signs of forced entry. The security cameras mysteriously turned off the afternoon of the burglary. The sheriff never filed a police report. His daughter, neighbors and the police think he's crazy. It was then that it dawned on me. The burglary never happened.

I learned that, despite Fred's alert and coherent demeanor, he was suffering from the very early stages of dementia. This medical information was confirmed by his daughter Andrea when I spoke with her the following morning. No wonder the police refused to file a report. Andrea said that her father had sold or given away the so-called stolen merchandise within the previous year. But as the weeks turned into months his medical condition caused him to forget. When he could no longer find the items in his home, Fred convinced himself he had been a victim of a burglary. The security video was blank, not due to some mysterious malevolent force. But because Fred had turned the machine off. He admitted that he did not know how to operate it correctly. He then filed a theft claim with his insurance company. He was very convincing because in his mind, the theft had occurred.

In the end, no charges were filed against him. I felt very sorry for Fred. He was a kind and gentle soul living alone on top of a mountain. He was struggling with the early stages of a long-term brain disease that would eventually rob him of all his precious memories. A very cruel and sad end to a long life.

Not all theft claims I investigated ended like Fred's. I once investigated an insurance claim filed by Mary Conroy which involved a missing diamond ring.

She wore a dazzling two-karat diamond wedding ring that sparkled like the sun at mid-day. The ring was a marquis-cut and worth close to three thousand dollars. She had filed an insurance claim on her homeowner's policy after losing the ring. I met Mary in her beautiful home in Olympus Cove, high up on the East Bench on the northwestern slope of Mount Olympus. We sat in her living room, which afforded visitors a commanding view of the entire Salt Lake Valley.

Mary was tall and thin and bore a striking resemblance to the late Karen Carpenter. She explained that her sister Beth from Portland had recently visited for the weekend. On Friday, Mary and Beth went shopping at City Creek Mall in downtown Salt Lake City. They had lunch in the food court, bought cosmetics at Lush, and tried on clothes at several department stores, eventually making a few purchases. Beth flew back to Portland the following Monday evening. It was after returning home from dropping Beth at the airport that Mary realized she wasn't wearing her diamond wedding ring. The last time she remembered wearing it was the previous Friday when she and Beth went shopping.

During my interview with Mary she stated that due to the size and cut of the ring she had taken it off while trying on outfits at the mall. She did so to avoid snagging it on the clothes. Mary believed she may have left it in one of the changing rooms. On the surface that seemed plausible. What didn't make sense to me is that she would go three days without realizing that her rather large wedding ring wasn't on her finger. Maybe a man would be that forgetful. But not a woman. And not with a ring that large. I just couldn't wrap my head around that fact. Furthermore, she hadn't even called any of the stores to ask about a lost ring. Mary had gone straight to the insurance company to file a claim. During my investigation, I also discovered she recently had the ring appraised. She presented me with copies of her original receipt of purchase and a copy of the appraisal.

After leaving Mary's home I went to the jewelry store in Sugar House where she had the ring appraised. I spoke with Sven, the owner and appraiser and showed him a copy of the appraisal Mary had given to me. He confirmed it was valid. And that was that. Or so I thought.

About two weeks later I was in my office opening up a new MacBook I had just purchased. As I began setting up my internet bookmarks, I decided out of the blue to check Mary's social media profiles. I observed several pictures of Mary and her family at what appeared to be a backyard bar-b-que from the previous weekend. And there was Mary smiling and waving to the camera, a large two-karat marquis cut diamond ring on her left hand.

I called the insurance company the next day to inquire as to whether they had paid the claim. Perhaps Mary had purchased an identical replacement. They had not yet settled the claim. I forwarded the adjuster a picture of Mary wearing the ring she had report missing. Or not missing, as it now appeared.

Notwithstanding the previous examples, thefts do occur. Something I discovered with the Case of the Missing Rebar.lxxxi It started out as most of my cases do, with a telephone call. By the time it was over I had nabbed the thieves and saved the client tens of thousands of dollars.

His name was Rod Steel and he owned a large construction company in West Valley City, Utah. He was going over the books one night in preparation for a regular audit by his accountant when he realized that something was off. Part of his business involved purchasing and using rebar to lay foundations at construction sites. There appeared to be a discrepancy in the amount of money he had paid for the rebar and the amount of rebar that was actually delivered to the various construction sites. Something nefarious was afoot.

I met him later the next day at his warehouse not far from the Salt Lake Airport. I got into the passenger side of his truck and he drove me around the warehouse grounds pointing out where the rebar was stored. He explained that it was loaded on to flatbed trucks and delivered to construction sites all along the Wasatch Front. I questioned him about his inventory control and everything seemed to be in order. The more he told me about it the more it began to look like an inside job. The rebar in question was 20 feet long. You don't just slip a 20-foot piece of steel into your back pocket and walk out to your car at the end of day. No, it had to be leaving the normal way. On the back of a truck. Whatever was happening to the rebar was happening after the trucks left the warehouse but before they arrived at the construction sites. One of his trusted employees was looting the company; peddling the metal, as it were. I told Rod what I needed, and we agreed to meet later that afternoon at a local Denny's restaurant near his warehouse.

In the meantime, I called my staff together and filled them in on the details. We would be following several flatbed trucks to multiple locations throughout the Salt Lake Valley to monitor what was happening to the rebar. On a good day, following someone is difficult. But following a large flatbed truck is especially difficult. You have to be close enough so you don't lose them but far enough away so you don't get made. One of the problems with these big rigs is that unless they're on the highway they're generally driving fairly slowly. Regardless of what you see on detective shows on television, slow drivers are burdensome to follow. They tend to notice everything around them. Slow truck drivers pay particularly close attention to their side mirrors as they make turns in a slow, sluggish manner. But we had no choice. We had to follow the trucks to find out what was happening to the rebar.

Later that same day I squeezed into a booth at Denny's and Rod handed me a beige manila folder containing all the information I had requested. I took a sip from my ice-cold Dr. Pepper and opened the folder finding a company check for my retainer. I immediately slipped it into my pocket. Included in the folder was a list of Rod's trucks and their license plates, color photographs of each assigned driver and a spreadsheet detailing this week's delivery schedule. I told Rod I'd be in touch and then slipped out the side entrance to the parking lot.

We got started the next day. It was a late summer in the Salt Lake Valley. Hot. Dusty. Unforgiving. The kind of day that made me long for the arrival of fall. We took up our surveillance positions near the warehouse and we waited. A short time later the trucks began pouring out of the warehouse grounds with their precious cargo. They took off in different directions each carrying about $15,000 worth of rebar. We each pulled in behind our assigned truck however they all went where they were supposed to go the first day. They delivered the correct amount of rebar to each site. It wasn't until the next day that we hit pay dirt.

We were in position again the next day when the trucks departed. All of the trucks stuck to their regularly scheduled stops again. All of the trucks that is, except two of them. They unexpectedly stopped at two unfamiliar construction sites. I double checked the spreadsheet Rod had given me at Denny's. I looked at the address I was at. It was definitely not on the list.

As the driver pulled in I grabbed my video camera and hit record. I watched as the driver unloaded a small portion of the rebar and received what appeared to be a cash payment from an unidentified man at the construction site. This driver, as well as one other, made a couple of unscheduled stops to sell rebar off the back of their trucks. We eventually discovered that an accomplice in the warehouse was adjusting the bills of lading to account for the missing rebar. We completed our investigation and turned our final report in to Rod. I'm not sure what became of the employees, as Rod told me he would handle it internally.

I had been making a somewhat comfortable living as a private investigator after my move from Missouri back to Texas in 2002. But by 2013 it became glaringly apparent that the competition was overwhelming. I was continually riding the tall peaks and low valleys of financial feast or famine. The unpredictability was no way to provide for a family. Texas, like Florida, California, New York and so many other large states, just had too many private investigators. To be successful in those large markets one had to specialize in a single type of investigation. While that made good business sense, I've never been that way. I've always had a desire to offer and work a variety of investigative specialties. Otherwise, I found boredom set in. Furthermore, although I love Texas, the heat and high humidity of what was essentially almost nine months of summer was particularly hard to deal with, especially because I spent so much of my time outdoors on surveillance. I would return home each afternoon drenched in sweat and physically exhausted from the heat. I had begun to consider other possible options.

Three decades earlier I had spent time as a Mormon missionary in western Montana and had fallen in love with the state. The natural beauty of the snow-caped rugged mountain peaks, green lush valleys and crystal-clear lakes were beyond compare. The people were friendly, and the pace of life was a bit slower. I had considered moving there for many years. I felt that Montana was where I could become a big fish in small private eye pond, so to speak. Unfortunately, the depressed wages and the long-drawn-out winter months precluded me from seeing that dream to fruition. More importantly, I could never talk Valerie into it. She was raised in Spokane which lies at about the same latitude. It was just too cold she said. Still, I longed for a place with low humidity and four seasons.

Over the years several members of my family, including three sisters and a niece had all relocated to Utah. There, in the shadow of the western edge of the Rockies, Utah had the same beautiful snow-capped mountains, low crime, an educated and friendly populace, and one of the highest median-household income levels in the U.S. It was a much smaller private investigation market than Texas. But I would be able to work the types of cases I wanted to work and be the proverbial big fish in a small pond.

There was also something enticing about the west. There was space there. And room to grow. The jagged and weathered mountains seemed to make time stand still. The cold and swiftly flowing rivers move along their hurried path with purpose and resolve. Even the people seemed different; determined, as if nothing was impossible. They embraced an attitude of minimal government intervention and maximum personal freedom.

I've always considered myself a city person. But as I've grown older I have found myself desiring a slower pace; more peace and quiet. There is also something about the intermountain west. I discovered a certain personal harmony and solace in the vast openness and the slower pace of life. A man could reinvent himself here. So, in October of 2013 we once again rented a truck and found ourselves on yet another move. This time, to the right place; to Salt Lake City, Utah, the crossroads of the west. It would be our last move.

CHAPTER 17

FULMER, P.I.

The move to Utah changed everything. Like the early Mormon pioneers that finally found peace and shelter from their enemies in the shadow of the Rocky Mountains, I finally achieved my dream. I would become a big fish in a small private eye pond and realize the lasting success that had somehow eluded me for so many years.

Utah was admitted to the union as the 45th state on January 4, 1896. It was settled almost forty years earlier on July 24, 1847, by members of the Church of Jesus Christ of Latter Day Saints, commonly referred to as Mormons. Like the early pilgrims seeking religious freedom, Mormon pioneers were fleeing religious persecution in Missouri and Illinois. As the persecution intensified, they began searching for a place where they could worship God and live their religion in peace.

On June 27, 1844, an angry mob of about one hundred men, their faces painted black with gun powder, stormed the second floor of a small brick jail in Carthage, Illinois. They forced their way through a wooden door at the top of the stairs and killed the Mormon Prophet, Joseph Smith and his brother Hyrum.

Afterwards, the religious persecution only intensified. In 1842, Joseph Smith had prophesied that the Latter-Day Saints would, "become a mighty people in the midst of the Rocky Mountains." Less than a year and a half after his martyrdom Brigham Young, like a modern-day Moses, began leading the Saints 1,300 miles across the great plains to the Salt Lake Valley.

At the time, Utah was a barren wilderness, home to the Ute Indian tribe and not much else. The treaty of Hidalgo Guadalupe was signed February 2, 1848 by the U.S. and Mexico, thus ending the Mexican-American War and making Utah a U.S. territory. The Mormon pioneers began settling communities up and down the Wasatch Front planting crops, digging irrigation ditches, constructing churches and temples and building a new life for themselves. I would find myself doing the same.

Now days, over three million people call Utah home. About eighty percent of the population reside up and down the Wasatch Front, a chain of neighboring cities from Nephi in the south all the way up to Brigham City in the north. Salt Lake City is in the middle and, like any large metropolitan area, has its problems. Homelessness, auto theft, prostitution, fraud and drugs. In fact, like most states it has been hit hard by heroin and prescription opiate addiction. More Utahns die from prescription drug overdoses each year than from car accidents.

One of my very first cases in Utah involve heroin, although it was actually a child custody case. Toni Nicholson was a short, thin mother of two that lived in North Salt Lake. She would cruise downtown Salt Lake City about every other day looking for Aunt Hazel, the street name for sticky black tar heroin. After scoring a single gram for twenty dollars from a dealer near Pioneer Park, Toni drove to a convenience store at the intersection of 500 South and 400 West and smoked it in the restroom. She then drove back to her upper-class home in North Salt Lake only to repeat the process a day later.

I had a GPS tracker attached to the underside of Toni's light blue Toyota Yaris. I also set up a geo-fence because I never knew when she would head downtown for drugs. A geo-fence is a virtual perimeter I set up in a wide radius around Toni's home and immediate neighborhood in North Salt Lake. She could leave her house and go to the grocery store, gym and her children's school without the GPS tracker alerting me. Which is good, because all I was interested in were her trips downtown for drugs. However, once she drove outside the prescribed radius of her North Salt Lake neighborhood I would receive a text alert informing me she was on the move. I could then watch her on my iPad and follow her every move as she proceeded to downtown Salt Lake City.

GPS trackers do not send alerts in real-time. But the ones I use are updated every two minutes. Add to that the need to refresh my iPad and then drive to her location, and I was always a few minutes behind her. I ended up following her downtown on seven different occasions. Six of those seven times I was able to obtain snippets of video of her. But I was never able to get her on video buying or using the drugs. She was just too fast. Sadly, things don't always happen the way they do in the movies.

Speaking of drugs, I was on a workers' compensation surveillance in the Kearns area watching a house on 5600 West. I had a clear view of the subject's home across an open field. At first, I didn't really notice the other home two houses down from my subject's residence. Nor did I initially observe the cars coming and going from that home. That is, until it became glaringly obvious. A car would pull up and someone would run in the home. They'd be inside for about two minutes then they'd run back out and the car would depart. This sinister activity would repeat itself all morning. Evidently, I was sitting near a drug dealer's house in Kearns while watching my insurance fraud claimant. While Utah and much of the U.S. struggled with a drug problem, Colorado added to it by legalizing recreational marijuana use in January of 2014.

One of my first cases in Colorado involved a very unique workers compensation claim. Jay Donovan, a young, thin, twenty-five-year-old with dreadlocks, had fallen and broken his arm at Pocobis Holdings, a cannabis manufacturing company in Longmont, Colorado. Donovan worked at Pocobis packaging cannabis edibles for distribution across the state. It was all fairly simple. Jay had come around the corner to talk with a co-worker in the extraction lab and slipped on the recently mopped floor.

I conducted interviews and took pictures of the accident site. I also got a tour of the facility from the manager. I don't use marijuana products, but I found the facility fascinating. It was very modern with chemists using high-tech laboratory equipment to extract the THC from the Cannabis plants and prepare it for use in a variety of products. I guess I expected to see employees in tie-die shirts rolling marijuana joints, but the facility was very modern producing over thirty different types of cannabis products.

I was once on a workers' compensation surveillance, this time in Brigham City, Utah. It was a sunny but cool fall morning. I could see the dried fallen leaves hurriedly whisked down the street by a gentle, invisible wind. A bright yellow school bus stopped nearby belching out that familiar diesel exhaust smell that always reminds me of my time in the Army. Several excited children in brightly colored coats and backpacks boarded the bus in single file. I heard the loud hiss of air pressure as the driver closed the door, released the brakes and departed the neighborhood. Somewhere in the distance I heard a child cry.

I was set up about three houses down from my subject's residence and had an excellent view of his front door and garage. I moved to the back seat of my van and adjusted my video camera's zoom setting ensuring that I would be prepared when the subject appeared. Again, I heard what sounded like a small child crying somewhere down the street, but I didn't give it much thought at the time. I'm a father of three and it wasn't my child, so I was somehow able to tune it out. Besides, I was waiting for my subject to exit his residence. But the crying persisted. It eventually dawned on me that the child was in distress. The crying seemed to emanate from the front of my vehicle on the left side. I moved toward the front seat of my van and looked out my driver's side window and that's when I saw Spider Man.

Obviously, I did not see Peter Parker outside my driver's side window. What I did see was a barefoot seven-year old boy in Spider Man pajamas standing in his front yard crying. I looked around, but I didn't see any adults or any vehicles in the driveway. The boy periodically walked towards the front door out of my view and then back to the front yard. I suspected that he had been left home alone, probably while he was asleep. When he awoke to find the house empty he must've walked outside and locked himself out of the house.

I immediately called the police and reported it. I then kept an eye on him until the police arrived. And in a rather serendipitous move, both his mother and a police cruiser arrived at the residence at the same time. The boy was safe. But his mother got an earful from the police officer about leaving such a small child home alone. I'm just glad the child didn't run off while I was watching him. I would've had to break off my surveillance. But Brooklyn was a runner. She was a teenager that participated in a 5k run, even though she claimed to have been injured in an auto accident.

Brooklyn was injured in a car accident although the accident was not her fault. Her father had contacted the insurance company and began the slow dance of negotiating a settlement for his daughter. But the days turned into weeks and the weeks turned into months. And suddenly, according to her father, the girl began to experience increasingly worse health, due to the accident. It was affecting every aspect of her life including her school work and her extra-curricular activities.

The father himself grew cantankerous and unpleasant to deal with. The adjuster grew more and more frustrated as time went on. It had been a simple car accident, yet Brooklyn's father refused to settle the claim. He was apparently holding out for a fortune.

I ended up spending only four hours on the investigation. But those four hours would end up saving the client several thousand dollars. In fact, I never even conducted surveillance at Brooklyn's house. I was able to develop a local confidential informant that knew the girl. And she provided some information early on that made all the difference. Brooklyn was on her high school track team. And they practiced several days a week.

I showed up one afternoon at Skyline High School, her school in Millcreek, Utah. I was able to surreptitiously shoot video of her during track practice. She wasn't particularly tall, but she had long legs that were lithe and quick. While I did get some video showing the girl engaging in activity outside the scope of her alleged injuries, I had difficulty getting a proper vantage point from which to shoot video. But it wasn't a total loss. Because I found out that in exactly 10 days Brooklyn was running a 5k in the Salt Lake City area.

It was early May and the weather was still relatively cool in the mornings. This particular 5k started at a local high school football stadium. The route went through the adjacent neighborhood and then eventually deposited the runners back where they started, at the stadium. That morning I sat in the stands with my video camera. Hiding in plain sight with two hundred other spectators. It took a few minutes to find her in the crowded mass of runners. But she was number forty-nine. She had on purple running shorts and a white Nike tank top. I shot video of her as she hopped up and down and then pulled each leg up behind her next to her buttocks. She then went into a pre-run stretching routine.

When you're a private eye there comes those moments before you begin filming a subject when you know you've nailed them. It's not a haughty feeling of superiority; at least it isn't for me. It's more of a realization that because you did your homework, because you were prepared, because you were in the right place at the right time – you're able to gather solid video that undeniably shows your subject has been dishonest. I take no pleasure in knowing that people lie or stretch the truth. In fact, I find it rather disconcerting. As private eyes, especially with insurance defense surveillance, we often deal in shades of grey. Half-truths. Half injury, half healthy. But with Brooklyn I was able to obtain incontrovertible evidence that she was faking her injury.

The starter pistol fired, and I stood up. I followed Brooklyn as she weaved a path through the runners and made her way to the front of the group. I kept the camera steadily fixed on her until she disappeared through the exit at the end of the stadium followed by the mass of other runners. I then sat down and waited for her return.

A short time later she reappeared at the stadium doors and I filmed her again as she sprinted the last fifty yards and completed the run. Her face was red. She was breathing heavy as she paced back and forth with her hands on her hips walking off the effects of the run. The girl's hair was a mess and the sweat on her skin glistened in the sunlight. She eventually caught her breath and began chugging down small Styrofoam cups of Gatorade. Obviously, there was nothing wrong with her. Perhaps it was her father's fault. I chose to believe that. I'm sure she was unfamiliar with the claims process. I'm sure she would run again in the future. But this was one race her father was going to lose. The only "cool down" he was going to experience was from the adjuster. She had his number and tomorrow was going to be his rest day.

Whether it's surveillance or taking a statement, it's important for a private investigator to be able to read body language. Tonya Reiman is a body language expert who has appeared on several news programs. She often is shown videos of politicians and celebrities and then asked to analyze their body language. Although some disregard the value of non-verbal communication I believe it has significant merit. In fact, a couple of studies conducted by Dr. Albert Mehrabian, a professor of Psychology at UCLA, found that communication can be boiled down to what he calls the 7%-38%-55% rule. Seven percent of our communication is verbal, in other words what we actually say. Thirty-eight percent is based on the tone of our voice. Anyone that's raised a teenager can understand that. The final fifty-five percent, the majority, is based on our actual body language when speaking. After almost thirty years in the business of watching people I think a lot can be learned from body language. The investigation of Frank Curtis is a perfect example.

After a stunningly mediocre career, Frank retired from his job in the transportation industry for a public utility in Salt Lake City. Shortly after announcing his upcoming retirement, Frank decided to follow through with one of the more common red flags associated with workers' compensation fraud. He allegedly injured his back during his last week at work. The accident occurred right before he was set to retire. This put Frank in line for possibly receiving a disability check along with his monthly retirement check. His claims adjuster, Ella Tate, discussed the case with me and then I ventured over to Frank's neighborhood to begin work.

I arrived in the early morning hours and set up my surveillance. As I sat all nestled in my vehicle waiting for some activity I noticed a large moving truck slowly plodding down the road in my direction. As a private investigator, I'm attune to anything out of the ordinary. The driver applied the brakes and came to a complete stop near Frank's house; the brakes squeaking and letting loose that familiar pop as the compressed air escaped. The driver then climbed down from the cab holding a clip board. He was accompanied by another worker who had been sitting in the passenger seat. They both then began walking up to Frank's front door. The Fulmer Luck had struck again, this time in Utah. My first day of surveillance on Frank and he was moving.

I learned later on that Frank was moving to St. George, Utah, a popular community for retirees. I grabbed my video camera and prepared to document his activities. The movers exited his house and I watched as they walked to the back of the truck. They raised the large back door and began lowering the ramp. For the next twenty minutes, they carried furniture and boxes out of the house, down the sidewalk and on to the truck. It was all very routine for them. Just another move. But somewhere during that time Frank made his first appearance. He was in his mid-sixties with wild unkempt white hair and a bushy moustache. He looked a lot like Albert Einstein. Frank was wearing blue jeans and a brown short-sleeved shirt. He seemed nervous and agitated. He fidgeted with his hands. He gave verbal instructions every time a mover walked out of his house with an item. If I had been one of the movers, my first thought would've been – this is going to be a long move.

Frank had gone to the trouble and expense of hiring professional movers. But one look at his body language and I could tell he'd rather do it himself. He continued to watch the movers. He repeatedly stopped them and gave them instructions as they carried his belongings to the truck. Frank was the poster child for "If you want something done right, do it yourself." I continued to focus my camera on him. I knew that despite his alleged bad back he would start picking up boxes. He just couldn't help himself. And then Frank made his move, so to speak.

Frank began carrying boxes out to his car. Many of the boxes Frank carried out were labeled "Fragile," meaning they were more than likely light-weight items. He placed them in the back of his small hatchback. I obtained video as he crawled on his hands and knees inside the car pushing the boxes close to the back of the front seats. Despite his alleged back injury, he just couldn't bring himself to sit there and do nothing. I saw it coming because I had recognized his body language. I spent the next forty-five minutes gathering video of Frank. He was like so many subjects from cases over the last thirty years, displaying behaviors that belied their supposed injuries. My video put the kibosh on Frank's double dipping retirement scheme.

Not all my cases have involved insurance fraud schemes. Some, like the case of Ellen, involved a scheming husband. Ellen lived in beautiful San Rafael, California, about twenty minutes from the Golden Gate Bridge and the trendy restaurants and boutiques of Sausalito. Her husband Lloyd worked in the oil industry and had spent much of the last five years working in the Uintah Basin area of eastern Utah. Lloyd returned home to San Rafael for about a week every couple of months. It was a brutal schedule, but he and Ellen did not have any children. Sadly, after thirty-five years of marriage they seemed to be drifting apart, each occupied by their own interests. The marriage appeared to have run its course. Ellen still held out hope that Lloyd would find a job in California and they would be able to return to how things used to be.

Ellen called me because she suspected her husband was seeing another woman. During the work week, he stayed at a hotel in Vernal, a small town in eastern Utah. But whenever she called Lloyd on the weekend he was in Salt Lake City. I told her how much my retainer was, and I heard an audible gulp on the other end of the line. She didn't understand why it would cost that much. I explained to her the distance, mileage and the time involved to conduct the investigation and follow him from Vernal to Salt Lake City, one hundred and seventy-three miles away. I added that things don't happen in real life like they do on television. Ellen wasn't willing to pay that much for the truth. I told her I could look into Lloyd's background for considerably less than it would conduct surveillance. That option seemed to appeal to her, so I moved ahead.

The next day I began my background check and discovered in short order that Lloyd was seeing another woman. In fact, he had recently married a woman named Hannah. She owned a house in Salt Lake City near the Hogle Zoo, presumably where Lloyd was living on the weekends. Of course, bigamy is illegal. Even in Utah. Something Ellen Greenwald discovered the hard way.

With my move to Utah I've been able to conduct a variety of types of investigations. My wife Valerie is a licensed Utah private investigator too, but she feels more comfortable working behind the scenes. I conduct the investigations and she handles the reports and the administrative details. She helps out with the investigations occasionally and so have other family members.

My sister Stephanie once helped Valerie and I follow a subject from Salt Lake City International Airport to his hotel in downtown Salt Lake across from Temple Square. Valerie kept the car running in the pickup lane while Steph and I sat in the airport. We had a picture of the subject and constantly scanned the crowd for his face. Trying to pick out a face in hundreds of arriving passengers can be difficult. But we got lucky this time and recognized him immediately. We got in step behind him and fortunately were able to follow him all the way to down town Salt Lake.

I once was asked what my business exit strategy was. That's easy. Death. I can't imagine doing anything else. I'll keep doing this as long as I can. In Raymond Chandler's epic novel, *The Long Goodbye*, private investigator, Philip Marlowe states, "*To say goodbye is to die a little.*"[lxxxii] And so, the investigations continue. Monday is different from Tuesday. One day I am flying to San

Francisco to investigate disability fraud. Next, I'm in Denver looking into a multi-million-dollar personal injury claim. Back in Utah I'm talking to a potential client about a year-old murder case. The police ruled it a suicide. But he thinks his mother was murdered. He claims to have proof. After a weekend home with my family, I'm off again to Houston, or Omaha, or Coeur d'Alene.

The work never ends. The emails keep coming and the phone continues to ring. A Hollywood producer calls. He has an idea for a reality show featuring a private investigator that tracks down heirs due an inheritance. An adjuster suspects a workers' compensation claimant in Boise is exaggerating her injuries. A middle-aged wife in Park City suspects her husband is cheating. One minute, a company calls needing proof a franchisee in Wyoming is violating their licensing agreement. The next, a father calls about his runaway daughter. She's been missing for two months. She was the star of her high school soccer team. She's pretty, with blue eyes and long blond hair. He thinks she may be in Las Vegas.

I sometimes feel strained. I see the worst in human nature. Cheating and lying. Fraud and greed. Assault and abuse. Sometimes it feels too heavy to bear, like a tremendous weight I can't get off my back. I grow weary of trying to come up with last minute practical solutions to other people's desperate problems. I'm tired of getting up before the crack of dawn. I spend so much time on surveillance in either the oppressive heat or the bitter cold. The ongoing stress of handling multiple investigations and the unrealistic expectations of clients can be emotionally exhausting. I am often by myself for days with no one to talk to. Sometimes I feel very alone. At other times, I just want to be left alone. I'm tired of people lying to rybody seems to want something from me. Money. Time. My advice. I feel stretched. As if there's not enough of me to go around. As if I'm giving hundred percent to everybody and it never seems to be enough. As if I alone, must carry the load. I need a break. I'm overdue for a vacation. I see myself lying on a quiet deserted beach far away from here. I close my eyes and I can feel the warm sunlight on my face. I hear the waves as they gently come and go. I feel perfectly relaxed and at peace. And then the phone rings and someone needs my help. And I find myself drawn back into the game again.

I do what I do because I have a desire to solve mysteries and to help people find closure and peace of mind. In many ways, I'm still that little blond-haired boy disappearing behind the library bookshelves to revel in the stories of mysteries solved. I've been fortunate enough in my life to make a living at what I love to do.

And so, time marches on. I'm ready for the next case, the next mystery, the next great adventure. I have an urge to get in the car and just drive. I'm singing, *Roll Me Away*[lxxxiii] with Bob Seger on the radio. I can see the impressive vastness of the West and the miles and miles of highway laid out before me. I see the rugged snow-capped mountain tops. I can see the Weber River and hear the rushing of the cold water as the current swiftly flows by. And then I am filled with excitement as I emerge from the narrow mouth of Weber Canyon and turn left, driving south on I-15 towards home. But after taking time off I feel that familiar urge again. The itch to travel. To go places. The need to help people find resolution. To solve problems. To make things right. I guess I'll always feel it. I don't think it will ever stop. The game is afoot, and I am ready.

ABOUT THE AUTHOR

Scott B. Fulmer is a licensed private investigator and the principal at Fulmer, P.I., a private investigation firm based in Salt Lake City, Utah. He has spent the last thirty years conducting investigations for state and federal government, as well as the private sector. Scott has a degree in criminal justice from the University of Texas at San Antonio and is a decorated combat veteran of the Gulf War. He lives somewhere in the mountains of Utah with his wife and children. This is his first book. For media inquiries, please contact him at scott@fulmerpi.com.

NOTES

i The National Center for Missing and Exploited Children (NCMEC), was founded by John and Revé Walsh after their son Adam was abducted in 1981. It is a clearinghouse for information about missing and abducted children.

ii *The Hardy Boys* is a fictional children's mystery series written by several ghost writers under the pseudonym of Franklin W. Dixon and first published in 1927.

iii *Encyclopedia Brown* is a fictional children's mystery series written by Donald J. Sobol and first published in 1963.

iv *Nancy Drew* is a fictional children's mystery series first published in 1930 and written by several ghost writers under the pseudonym Carolyn Keene.

v *The Three Investigators* is series of juvenile detective books written from 1964 to 1987. The stories were created and originally written by Robert J. Arthur.

vi *The Rockford Files* was so popular the television network would go on to produce eight Rockford Files made-for-TV-movies from 1994 to 1999.

vii Closed cases are cases no longer being actively investigated by law enforcement.

viii Pro bono is short for pro bono publico, a Latin phrase meaning *for the public good*; meaning free.

ix Whataburger is a privately held fast food hamburger chain.

x *The Six-Million Dollar Man* moniker was as reference to a television show of the same name that appeared on ABC from 1974 through 1978. The series starred Lee Majors as a Steve Austin, an astronaut who, after an accident, was given bionic implants that gave him super powers.

xi Christian Brando was the son and only child of academy-award winning actor Marlon Brando and his ex-wife Anna Kashfi, with whom he was involved in a bitter child custody dispute. Christian was reportedly kidnapped in March of 1972. Brando hired private investigator Jay J. Armes who eventually discovered the child in Mexico. Years later, Christian pled guilty to fatally shooting the boyfriend of his half-sister Cheyenne. He was also a suspect in the murder of Bonnie Blakely.

xii *Breakout* was a 1975 Columbia Pictures film starring Charles Bronson and his real-life wife, actress Jill Ireland. In the film, a businessman named Wagner is incarcerated in a Mexican prison and his wife hires Bronson's character, Nick Colton, to rescue him. Colton flies into the prison courtyard in a helicopter, rescues Wagner and flies back across the U.S.-Mexico border to Brownsville, Texas.

xiii The MEPS (Military Entrance Processing Station), is where all new military recruits enter the service.
xiv BDU or Battle Dress Uniform, was the standard U.S. Army utility uniform worn from the early 1980's until the mid-2000's.
xv The 7th Cavalry Regiment was formed July 28, 1866 and participated in the American Indian Wars. The regiment's band adopted the Irish tune "*Garryowen*" as their march tune. Much of the 7th Cavalry Regiment was decimated at the Battle of Little Bighorn between Gen. George A. Custer and the Lakota chief Sitting Bull. Years later the regiment saw action in World War Two and the Vietnam Conflict, as well as operations Desert Storm, Iraqi Freedom and Enduring Freedom.
xvi The Battle of Ia Drang Valley occurred November 14th through November 18th, 1965 in Vietnam. It was the first major conflict between U.S. forces and the North Vietnamese Army (NVA). The battle is described in painstaking detail in the book *We Were Soldiers Once, and Young* by General Harold G. Moore and Joseph L. Galloway. Moore commanded the unit during the battle. Galloway, a civilian UPI reporter from Refugio, Texas, was embedded with the unit at the time. I had an opportunity to meet Galloway in 1990 when he traveled to Saudi Arabia and met with my unit, the 1st/7th Cavalry Regiment. Galloway was in country from 1990 to 1991 to cover the 24th Infantry Division (Mechanized) assault into Iraq.
xvii The M113 is a track-mounted armored personnel carrier first used by U.S. Army mechanized infantry during the Vietnam War.
xviii The Wadi Al-Batin is a dry river bed that runs about 45 miles northeast from Saudi Arabia into Kuwait. It serves as the border between Iraq and Kuwait.
xix Clausewitz, Carl von; Howard, Michael, Editor and translator; Paret, Peter, Editor and translator (1989) [1832]. *On War*. Princeton, NJ: Princeton University Press.
xx NATO (North Atlantic Treaty Organization or the North Atlantic Alliance), is a 28-country military and government alliance formed in 1949.
xxi Reforger (REturn FORces to GERmany) was an annual joint military exercise conducted by NATO forces from 1969 through 1993.
xxii Ricks College, in Rexburg, Idaho, transitioned from a two-year college to a four-year university in 2001 and renamed Brigham Young University – Idaho.
xxiii MOS or Military Occupational Specialty. All jobs in the military are assigned a nine-digit identification code. I was an 11C, an indirect fire infantryman (mortars).
xxiv CID is the abbreviation for the U.S. Army Criminal Investigation Command. They investigate violations of the Uniform Code of Military Justice.
xxv The rivalry between the University of Texas and Texas A&M University ended in 2011 when Texas A&M left the Big 12 Conference.
xxvi Connolly, John; 2006. *The Book of Lost Things*. Atria Books.
xxvii Being "burned" or "made" in private investigator vernacular means that the subject has become aware of the surveillance.
xxviii A one-percenter is reference to an alleged comment by the American Motorcyclist Association that 99% of those who ride motorcycles are law abiding citizens. The implication being that the remaining 1% are outlaws. Consequently, motorcycle clubs such as the Hell's Angles, Mongols and Bandidos are known as one percenters.

xxix A bar back assists a bartender behind the bar doing everything but serving drinks, i.e. restocking the cooler, replacing spirits, cleaning, replacing ice, etc.

xxx A Mexican Charro Suit is a decorative outfit traditionally worn by Mexican cowboys and Mariachis.

xxxi Asperger's Syndrome (AS), now categorized as High-Functioning Austism, is a neurobiological disorder on the higher-functioning end of the Austim spectrum.

xxxii Saddam Hussein used chemical weapons on both, the Kurds and on Iran during the Iran-Iraq War from 1980 until 1988; two years before the Gulf War.

xxxiii MOPP stands for *Mission Oriented Protected Posture*. It is the protective gear donned by U.S. military personnel to prevent injury during a nuclear, biological or chemical attack.

xxxiv Loss of Consortium stipulates an injury has deprived the subject of familial benefits, such as an inability to provide affection or engage in sexual activity.

xxxv Occam's Razor is a theory postulated by theologian and philosopher William of Ockham. It states that among competing explanations for a problem, the simplest explanation is often the most likely.

xxxvi A Bull Float is used to spread cement evenly across a large area.

xxxvii Credit headers are at the top of a credit report and contain basic non-credit information such as the subject's name, address, social security number, etc. This information is not protected by the Fair Credit Protection Practices Act.

xxxviii A VIN is a Vehicle Identification Number. Each vehicle has a unique 17-digit VIN to positively identify a vehicle for insurance, warranty and theft purposes.

xxxix *Chicago* was written by Carl Sandburg, and first published in *Poetry* in 1941.

xl OPM (Office of Personnel Management), is a government agency that manages the U.S. civil service, including recruiting personnel.

xli A PR (Periodic Reinvestigation) is required every five years to maintain a top-secret security clearance.

xlii OPM still maintains offices in the cave, but it has since been purchased by Iron Mountain, a record management company based out of Boston, Massachusetts.

xliii FPS (Federal Protective Service) is the police division of the U.S. Department of Homeland Security. FPS provides security for over 9,000 government buildings owned or leased by the General Services Administration of the U.S. Government.

xliv The GRiD Compass was one of the first laptop computers. They were manufactured by the GRiD Systems Corporation and used by the OPM's OFI.

xlv NASA is responsible for the U.S. space program as well as aerospace research.

xlvi Passed in 1955, the Act arranges for the construction of presidential libraries to house presidential documents. Financing is through private donations.

xlvii NARA (National Archives and Records Administration), is a government tasked with preserving all of the documents and records of the U.S. government.

xlviii C-SPAN is a public affairs network that broadcasts U.S. political events.

xlix Panetta was CIA director under President Obama and then Secretary of Defense.

l Kasich became governor of Ohio and then ran for the U.S. Presidency in 2016.

li DOE (Department of Energy), manages nuclear material and reactors.

lii A one megawatt rating indicates a nuclear reactor with an output of 1 million watts. This is a small reactor used primarily for training purposes.

liii A Q clearance is a security clearance granted by the DOE.

liv FMC is a Federal Medical Center; essentially a prison hospital

lv Carswell AFB was selected for closure in 1990 by the BRAC commission and was renamed Naval Air Station Ft. Worth Joint Readiness Base.

lvi Lynette "Squeaky" Fromme, a member of the Manson Family; attempted to assassinate President Gerald R. Ford in 1975.

lvii John Wesley Hardin was an old west outlaw and gunfighter

lviii Duane "Dog" Chapman is a bounty hunter and star of the popular television reality shows "*Dog the Bounty Hunter*" and "*Dog and Beth: On the Hunt*".

lix Carrasco was a South Texas drug kingpin incarcerated at the Walls in Huntsville, Texas. In 1974, Carrasco and two other inmates took hostages at the Walls Unit in an attempt to escape. He was consequently shot and killed.

lx The Missouri State Penitentiary in Jefferson City, Missouri was the oldest operating prison west of the Mississippi River. It served as the state's maximum-security prison from 1836 until its closure in 2004. Inmates have since been transferred to the new Jefferson City Correctional Center.

lxi Exculpatory evidence is evidence favorable to the defendant that tends to exonerate them of the crime.

lxii The PRSI or Personal Subject Interview is a detailed personal interview that verifies information from the SF 86 and serves as the main type of interview to obtain a U.S. government security clearance.

lxiii The U.S. Public Health Service is a uniformed division of the U.S. Department of Health and Human Services. The service promotes and advances the public health

lxiv SF-86 or Standard Form 86 is a detailed questionnaire for those applying for employment positions with the U.S. government that require a national security clearance.

lxv Formerly known as the White House Police, the Uniformed Division is a division within the U.S. Secret Service of uniformed police officers that protect the physical grounds of the White House and several other buildings in the Washington, D.C. area, including foreign diplomatic missions.

lxvi Coyotaje, or the more common spelling of Coyote, is a colloquial Spanish term in Mexico that refers to an individual who smuggles illegal immigrants across the Texas-Mexico border for a fee, typically between $1,500.00 and $2,500.00 per person.

lxvii The U.S. Immigration and Naturalization Service, or INS, was dissolved on March 1, 2003 when the agency came under the auspices of the new U.S. Department of Homeland Security. The INS' responsibilities were divided among three new government agencies, including the U.S. Citizenship and Immigration Services (USCIS); the U.S. Immigration and Customs Enforcement (ICE) and the U.S. Customs and Border Protection (CBP).

lxviii Malingering is a workers' compensation term meaning to exaggerate or fake an injury in order to avoid returning to work.

lxix The U.S. Bureau of Engraving and Printing is part of the U.S. Department of Treasury and the government agency responsible for printing U.S. currency. The Ft. Worth facility is responsible for printing about half of all U.S. currency.

lxx The NRO or National Reconnaissance Office was founded in 1961 and up until September 18, 1992, the very existence of this branch of the intelligence community, including the name of the organization, was classified top secret. The organization works with defense contractors in the private sector to both design and construct satellites and other space reconnaissance systems to monitor the communications of foreign intelligence targets.

lxxi NSA Hawaii (NSAH), often referred to as "The Tunnel," is one of five U.S. cryptologic sites that monitor signals intelligence (SIGINT), more specifically the communications of foreign intelligence targets, to protect U. S. interests

lxxii A Qui Tam lawsuit is a whistleblower lawsuit; where an employee reveals misconduct, fraud or corruption being conducted by the employer.

lxxiii Deus ex Machina is Latin for *god from the machine*. It refers to when something previously viewed as unsolvable is suddenly solved by the last-minute intervention of a person or object.

lxxiv *Marley and Me: Live and Love with the World's Worst Dog*, is a 2005 New York Times bestseller by journalist John Grogan. It tells the autobiographical story of the thirteen years they spent with their family pet, Marley, a yellow Labrador Retriever.

lxxv California v. Greenwood was the 1988 U.S. Supreme Court ruling stating that there was no expectation of privacy for discarded items, thus allowing private investigators (or anyone else) to engage in dumpster diving.

lxxvi According to the National Safety Council, about 7,000 people drown each year with 80% of the drownings occurring in residential swimming pools.

lxxvii *Anna Karenina* is an 1878 novel written by Russian author Leo Tolstoy. It was previously released as a serial in the periodical, *The Messenger*, from 1873 to 1877.

lxxviii The FBI generally only becomes involved in a kidnapping if the child is 12 years of age or younger, or there is an interstate aspect to the kidnapping.

lxxix *Farewell, My Lovely*, is a 1940 novel written by author Raymond Chandler featuring his fictional Los Angeles Private Investigator Philip Marlowe.

lxxx From Raymond Chandler's 1940 novel, *Farewell, My Lovely*.

lxxxi Reinforcing bar, or "Rebar," is a thick, long-tempered steel reinforcing rod commonly used in construction to strengthen and hold concrete together.

lxxxii *The Long Goodbye* is a 1953 novel by Raymond Chandler featuring the exploits of fictional Los Angeles Private Investigator, Philip Marlowe.

lxxxiii *Roll Me Away* is the title of a 1983 song written by Bob Seger on his album, *The Distance*.

Printed in Great Britain
by Amazon